LANSING
—— AND THE ——
CIVIL WAR

MATTHEW J. VANACKER

THE
History
PRESS

Published by The History Press
Charleston, SC
www.historypress.com

Front cover: *Birds Eye View of the City of Lansing, Michigan 1866*, by A. Ruger and Chicago Lithographing Co. *Library of Congress, https://www.loc.gov/item/73693436/.*

First published 2023

Manufactured in the United States

ISBN 9781467149198

Library of Congress Control Number: 2022947090

Notice: The information in this book is true and complete to the best of our knowledge. It is offered without guarantee on the part of the author or The History Press. The author and The History Press disclaim all liability in connection with the use of this book.

To those who kept the home fires burning, to those who did not return and to those who departed as boys and came home changed and often haunted men.

Contents

Preface

I am a son of Lansing, having had what I have always considered to be the great fortune of being born and raised in Michigan's capital city. My family lived and worked in the long morning shadow of our grand statehouse, and the city became an important part of who and what I am. The pride I hold in my hometown was fueled by the time my family spent in downtown Lansing, and my lifelong interest in the Civil War began with a visit to the state capitol.

My mother and father moved to Lansing from their family farms in Westphalia and Winn, Michigan, shortly after World War II. My mother and a few close friends rented a home on Shiawassee Street, and she worked as a front desk clerk at the Hotel Olds—directly across from the state capitol. My father lived with an older sister and her family in north Lansing on Sheridan Road near his new job at the Motor Wheel Corporation, where he would spend the next thirty-eight years. My parents met through the auspices of the young adult club of St. Mary's Cathedral downtown, a courtship briefly interrupted by my father's two years of military service during the Korean War. Shortly after my father's return from duty overseas, my parents married and bought their first home on South Pennsylvania Avenue, just south of Potter's Park Zoo, where they started their family. Eventually, the family of seven children outgrew the home on South Penn, and my parents bought a new home just west of the city in the burgeoning suburb of Delta Township.

Downtown Lansing, however, was always the focal point of our activities as a family. Downtown was where we shopped, dined and viewed parades on the Fourth of July and Veterans Day. It was where we saw the latest movies in one of the numerous downtown theaters. Visits to Dr. Spencer's office downtown were often augmented with trips to the department stores on Washington Avenue. The anticipated fall opening of school solicited the mandatory trip downtown to purchase school clothes, shoes and scout uniforms, either at J.C. Penney, J.W. Knapps or Arbaughs Department Store, often with a stop at D&C's five-and-dime on Saginaw Street. Christmas found our family again visiting downtown to view the beautiful window displays. If my mother was feeling especially solicitous, these trips would consist of riding the department store escalators (the first and last steps were always filled with anxiety), a sojourn to the Peanut Shop and—if we had been especially well-behaved—lunch of grilled cheese and tomato soup at one of the numerous downtown lunch counters.

These trips downtown always included, at the very least, a drive by the 1879 Michigan state capitol or perhaps a stroll on the capitol grounds to view the Civil War memorials and monuments. An especially memorable Civil War monument was dedicated to and erected by the First Michigan Volunteer Sharpshooters Regiment in October 1915. The monument, depicting a soldier perched behind a boulder, weapon at the ready, made a lasting impression upon many young lads, whose heads were filled with glory and dreams of serving in the armed forces one day. Little did I realize then the incredible sacrifice and personal pain the soldiers who fought for this regiment had endured, among them many boys from Lansing.

Occasionally, we would venture from the capitol grounds and enter the building. One of my very earliest childhood memories was a tour of the state capitol. Being the youngest child, I was often a tagalong on my older siblings' adventures and field trips. On this occasion, my mother, being a civic-minded citizen and dutiful den mother, arranged a field trip of the capitol for my older brother's Cub Scout den. I vividly recall standing in the central rotunda of the capitol surrounded by the smoke-begrimed, battle-scarred, bullet-torn and bloodstained flags our noble Michigan volunteers bore into combat and fought, bled and died beneath on the horrific battlefields of the great American Civil War. In hindsight, I am quite certain at that tender age I could not have possibly comprehended the magnitude of the service and sacrifice those torn banners represented. Even so, I found the experience to be humbling, remarkable and very, very memorable. I was four years old. Never could I have imagined that many years later, I would be charged with the responsibility of caring for those battle flags.

In my role as the director of the State Capitol Tour, Education and Information Service and in my capacity as a historian, one of my responsibilities has become the conservation of these truly remarkable artifacts. The 240 flags in the Michigan State Capitol battle flag collection have their way of deeply affecting a person. Gazing upon the battle honors lovingly inscribed, the blurred and shrunken stars, the stitching of the soldiers' own desperate attempts at battlefield repairs, the shattered staffs, the frayed fringe, the crimson-stained silk is an incredibly powerful experience. The flags have become to me as dear old friends, ragged, worn, aged, tired—so very, very tired—but desirous still of the opportunity to tell their stories. Desirous still, in their own infirmity, as old friends often are, to have someone—to have anyone—listen. Though alas, sadly, the flags do not—nay, they cannot—speak in audible tones, but their stories of undaunted courage and unimaginable bravery are manifested in their rent folds and their silken fields of glory.

Serving as the curator and caretaker of this collection is a responsibility I do not shirk, an honor I do not take lightly. These flags have become an important, almost essential, part of who I am as an individual and proud Michigander and who I am as an American. Therefore, the proceeds from the sale of this book are dedicated to the preservation of those flags and the erection of a Michigan monument at the Antietam National Battlefield honoring those Michigan men, including men from Lansing, who fought and there gave the last full measure of devotion.

The flags and the ninety thousand Michigan men, many from Lansing, who fought beneath them are now as mute as the grave, and so it becomes the responsibility of the living to ensure their stories are remembered. I believe the very best historians and authors are, at heart, storytellers. Who among us does not fully appreciate a well-told tale? This book is a humble attempt to tell the story of Lansing and the citizens of the city during the Civil War. It is a collection of tales, many that have not been told in recent times, both of Lansing during the war and the young men, our friends and neighbors from long ago, who left their homes and hearth fires in the capital city between 1861 and 1865 and, as Oliver Wendell Holmes Jr. wrote, "shared the incommunicable experience of war," for in their youths, their hearts were indeed "touched with fire."

For information or to support the Michigan Capitol Battle Flags or the Michigan at Antietam Monument project, please visit http://capitol.michigan.gov/SaveTheFlags/ and https://www.facebook.com/michigancivilwarassociation/.

Acknowledgements

In May 2020, I received an email from John Rodrigue, the Michigan acquisitions editor for The History Press, inquiring if I might be interested in writing a book. My first inclination was to submit to my inner fear and decline the invitation. I knew the subject was important and no other work had been published, to my knowledge, exclusively about Lansing during the Civil War, so this fear did not have as its origin the strength of the proposal itself but more the shortcomings of the author. My fear was not of my own personal failure but lay in my concern I would not do justice to the incredible sacrifices made by the city and her citizen soldiers during the Civil War. They so deserved to have their story told. I immediately thought of at least half a dozen more qualified and much more gifted authors who should write the book. When I voiced this concern to a friend and fellow historian, she said, "If not you, then who, and when?" After considerable mental and emotional turmoil and after talking it over with my very supportive wife and children, I put together the proposal for the book you are now reading.

There are so very many people to thank for the assistance they have offered on this journey to publication. Thank you to my editors, John Rodrigue and Zoe Ames, for taking a risk on a new author and offering support and assistance from start to finish. Thank you to my friends and colleagues at the State Capitol Tour, Education and Information Service and capitol historian and curator Valerie Marvin. They, along with our dedicated volunteer guides, are all top-notch educators and historians who have dedicated themselves to sharing their vast knowledge of Michigan's and its capitol's history with the citizens of our state. Thank you to the members and staff of the Michigan Capitol Commission and executive director Rob Blackshaw, for the constant and unquestioning professional support they have offered to me and my colleagues.

Thank you to Kerry Chartkoff, who has been my boss, my mentor and my chair and cochair of Save the Flags and, perhaps most importantly—my good friend. I owe my current position as the director of the Capitol Tour and Education Service and as curator of Save the Flags to Kerry. Thank you to Jerry Lawler, who encouraged me to apply, and then hired me for my first position at the state capitol. Jerry's dream was to write a definitive history of the city of Lansing, but sadly, he left this world far too early for his dream of publishing to come to fruition. His thorough research has assisted me greatly, and his loss is still keenly felt. Jerry, our hallowed halls still echo with your laughter.

My deepest appreciation to Jacob McCormick, Dan Miller, Scott Shattuck and Brian White, who generously shared images of Lansing soldiers and citizens; your generosity and assistance will not soon be forgotten. Thank you to historians Timothy Bowman, Bill Castanier, Jack Dempsey, Lille Foster, Jesse Lasorda, Margaret O'Brien and Craig Whitford: your edits, suggestions, information and photos have made this book all the better. Thanks also to my colleagues and friends serving with the Michigan Civil War Association: your quest to bring to light Michigan's important role in the Civil War is inspiring. Any and all omissions or inaccuracies are mine alone.

Finally, I would like to thank my late parents, John and Catherine; my extended family; my wife, Mary Kathleen; and my children, who have all been an incredible source of pride, strength, support, guidance and encouragement. Without you, I am nothing.

Introduction

For be it remembered that our little city had sent forth many, very many, bright, brave boys—all of whom had done their full duty and had given their "full measure of devotion" to our country and to its flag.[1]
—Seymour Foster

L ansing was at the time of the Civil War (1861–65)—and in many aspects continues to be—a relatively small community. The population of the city, according to the 1860 census, was approximately three thousand; this was a city where six degrees of separation could arguably be reduced to one or two. This small-town sentiment was still evident years after the conclusion of the Civil War when longtime Lansing resident and Civil War veteran Allen Shattuck stated, "There were not so many of us here in those days and a stranger was a curiosity. We were just plain 'Bill,' and 'Hank.' Everybody knew his neighbor's business and his given name."[2] This was especially true in comparison to other, much larger, metropolitan areas of Michigan, such as Detroit, whose 1860 population was over forty-five thousand, and Grand Rapids, whose population was twice that of Lansing's. This disparity was even more profound in comparison to other, more populous U.S. capital cities of the same period. In 1860, Columbus, Ohio, and Indianapolis, Indiana, both boasted populations of over eighteen thousand, while Albany, New York, had over sixty-two thousand citizens.[3]

The small population of Lansing, however, contributed to the overriding feeling of community. This was a place where people knew and, to a very large extent, attempted to care for one another—political, economic, religious and social differences aside. Longtime resident and mayor of Lansing Joseph Warner wrote, "We were one happy family. No jealousies, no social distinction—all seemed united in the one great object of building up a city."[4] This obviously prejudiced opinion of a city leader should not lead one to assume, however, that Lansing did not see and experience its fair share of strife, crime, struggles for justice and equality and political disagreements, as demonstrated by the two competing and very political newspapers published in the city, the *Lansing State Republican* and the opposing, democratic *Michigan State Journal*.

Seymour Foster enlisted in 1864 with the Second U.S. Sharpshooters Regiment, Company B, and postwar was very active in the Charles T. Foster Post of the Grand Army of the Republic. *Collection of Lille Foster.*

Among Lansing's greatest challenges, however, was and continues to be its own internal and eternal struggle to take its rightful place in the pantheon of capital cities. Lansing became the capital city of Michigan in 1847, after much haggling in the state legislature, which was then meeting in Detroit. Many cities were in competition to be named the new capital, and in the end, Lansing was offered as a compromise location, in part due to its central geographic location and the fact that the site was far from the border; the threat of British invasion, although greatly reduced, still loomed in the minds of many Michiganders. "It is indeed surprising that this site was selected," writes historian Jerry Lawler. "The State Census of 1845 gives the white population of Lansing Twp. as 88 souls, and the entire 36 square miles was practically an unbroken wilderness covered with virgin timber. The only settlement being a group of log cabins around a small sawmill at the east end of the dam at what is now North Lansing. Roads were mere trails through the woods which in the Spring and Fall were almost impassable. It is no wonder that the prediction was freely made that the whole thing was a huge joke and the bill would be repealed by the next Legislature."[5] Writes J.P. Edmonds in his *Early Lansing History*, "Many dire threats were made to have the Capital moved to some more civilized place as soon as they could get votes enough to do so."[6]

Lansing was very cognizant of the precariousness of its situation as the capital city, and great effort was expended in promoting favorable comparisons to other Michigan cities, foremost among them Detroit. In the fall of 1860, William Seward, who had recently been in contention for the Republican nomination for president, visited Lansing, and the town, recognizing it was on full display and vulnerable to critics, spared no expense to welcome him. The *Lansing State Republican*, quoting a *New York Times* correspondent, reported, "Detroit, the metropolis, was outdone by Lansing, the Capital."[7] The *Republican* also included a report from an Ohio correspondent who wrote glowingly of the event and the city, "The location of Lansing is a beautiful one…built upon the fine bluffs on the banks of the Grand River."[8]

In the midst of the war, and the January annual convening of the legislature, a correspondent for the democratic *Detroit Free Press*, as quoted by The *Republican*, wrote, "all Lansing lives out of the State and the sessions of the Legislature and that at best the hotels are but miserable one horse concerns….They take advantage of the necessities of men who are compelled to come here."[9] In defense of the city, the editor of the *Republican* countered that but a small number of Lansing men were employed by the state and that the citizens freely opened their doors to visitors, including legislators, accommodating their needs, due to the lack of hotel rooms, at a very reasonable rate. The *Republican* went on to assert that the hotels in Lansing offered "competition with those of any other city or village in the State…and furnish as good cheer generally, as can be found even in the hotels in Detroit."[10]

When the war came, Lansing was a city struggling to create its own identity, as well as the commercial, political, social and religious institutions and the basic infrastructure necessary to support the honor and great responsibility of having been designated as the capital city of Michigan. This struggle was only exacerbated by the Civil War and the essential military, financial and personal contributions necessary to help win and end it.

Chapter 1

GOOD BOYS, TRUE TO GOD AND COUNTRY

The Third Michigan Volunteer Infantry Regiment, Company G

In the early morning hours of April 12, 1861, Confederate artillery surrounding Fort Sumter in Charleston Harbor, South Carolina, began firing upon the island fortress and the besieged Union garrison. The echoes of these first guns of the American Civil War were felt across the country in faraway places, including Lansing. Following the attack upon Fort Sumter and President Lincoln's April 15 call for seventy-five thousand volunteers to put down the rebellion, numerous rallies and mass meetings were held. The records differ as to when the first Lansing rally was held, although some claim it was as early as the day after the attack on Sumter. On April 18, a large evening war rally was held in the Hall of Representatives at the capitol by "all those, without distinction of party, who love their country and honor its Flag and Constitution, to come to the rescue in this hour of danger and trial."[11]

Seymour Foster recorded his remembrances of one of those first rallies. Seymour, who would see action late in the war with a Lansing-based company of the Second U.S. Sharpshooters Regiment, recalled how all of Lansing turned out for a mass rally in "representative hall." The hall was very crowded, and many could not get in, so young boys, including Seymour, scrambled up the exterior walls to peer inside by perching precariously on the windowsills. In the hall, cheer after cheer greeted speech after fiery speech. Excitement rose to a fever pitch when it was announced a roll had been prepared and volunteers could come forward to sign up to fight for the Union. A sudden hush fell. Not a soul moved. Finally, Seymour recalled, he could just see someone was attempting to work his way through the crowd to the front. He couldn't tell who it was. Then a voice rang out: "Charles Foster tenders his services and his life if need be to his country and his flag."[12] Seymour's only brother, seven years his senior, had just become one of the first men from the capital city to enlist. A great cheer went up, and others shouldered forward to volunteer.

Charles T. Foster, who was twenty-three when he enlisted, was a clerk in Turner's Dry Goods Store. According to Seymour, he had a light complexion; big blue eyes; a beautiful singing voice, which he used to great effect in the Presbyterian choir and a "very becoming young mustache… with a genial disposition and agreeable manner, he was a general favorite with all who knew him."[13] Charles, who for a time had attended the new Michigan Agricultural College in East Lansing and had traveled west as far as Pikes Peak, Colorado, was the eldest of three children of Theodore and Frances Foster. The Foster family moved to Lansing in 1855 from Scio Township, Michigan, where Theodore had been a conductor on the Underground Railroad and the editor of the state's leading abolitionist newspaper, the *Signal of Liberty*, published in Ann Arbor. In 1855, the first Republican governor of Michigan, Kinsley Bingham, signed the law to establish a "House of Correction for Juvenile Offenders" at Lansing. Theodore Foster was appointed to the office of building commissioner for the state reform school and was then elected superintendent. In 1859, he built a home at 317 North Chestnut Street, where it still stands, very near the current capitol. During his time in Lansing, from 1855 to 1865, Theodore served at various times as superintendent of the reform school, city clerk, deputy collector of internal revenue and the editor of the *Lansing State Republican*.[14]

The majority of the first recruits from Lansing were members of the Williams Rifles. The Rifles was one of approximately twenty-five quasi–state supported militia groups functioning throughout Michigan before the war.[15] Some of these groups were military in name only and operated more as clubs, but when war came, they served as readymade companies that populated the early regiments. The Williams Rifles, named after their first commander, Adolphus Williams, was an armed and uniformed unit and would constitute the core of Company G of the Third Michigan Infantry Regiment. The group was "composed principally of hardy, muscular young men, farmer's sons who [were] accustomed to the use of the rifle and spoiling for a fight."[16] These men were friends. They were from the same city, they attended the same schools and churches,

Charles T. Foster was credited by some sources as being the first man from Lansing to enlist and the first Lansing soldier killed in action in the Civil War. *Collection of Lille Foster.*

they worked together and many of them were related to each other. The company was very much a familial organization. Among these blood relatives were members of the Shattuck family of Lansing.

Asa and Adaline Shattuck moved to Lansing from Washtenaw County in 1840. Captain Shattuck, as he was popularly known, supported his family of five boys and one daughter as a "mover of buildings." In 1861, Shattuck, along with his eldest son, Daniel, enlisted in the First U.S. Sharpshooters Regiment, Company C. Daniel was twenty-three; Asa was fifty-six. John Wiser, who may have been working as an apprentice to Asa and was living with the family, signed the Company C muster roll at the same time. Three other sons would also see action in the war. In 1861, Allen Shattuck enlisted with Company G, Third Michigan Infantry, on the same day as his friend Charles T. Foster, and one year later, his younger brother Nelson joined them in the field. In 1862, both Daniel and Asa were disabled and discharged from the service; little doubt Asa's advanced age contributed to his disability discharge. A few months later, Daniel reenlisted to join his brothers with the Third Infantry. In 1864, one of the youngest Shattuck boys, Edgar, enlisted with Company A, Eighth Michigan Volunteer Infantry Regiment. One can only imagine the anguish of Adaline, having her husband and four of her five boys away from home and engaged in combat.[17] Two of her boys would return to Lansing severely wounded, and another would spend his final days in a Confederate prisoner of war camp.

By April 24, forty-nine Lansing men, in addition to the original forty-three members of the Williams Rifles, had signed the muster roll to join what would eventually become Company G. Included in this roster of men were Sergeant Jerome Ten Eyck, who would end the war as a brevet major of U.S. Volunteers, and Sergeant Homer Thayer. Twenty-two-year-old Thayer was a First Ward merchant and made his living as a notary public and land agent while his young wife, Julia, taught music.[18] Thayer would fight through the entire war, including service in D.C., where he attended Ford's Theater on the fateful evening of April 14, 1865, and became a witness to the assassination of President Lincoln. He also served on the western frontier, where he and his wife settled before eventually moving back home to Lansing. Thayer would muster out of military service in 1867 as a brevet major of U.S. Volunteers.

Among the other Lansing men who enlisted that spring day in 1861 were John Broad and Eli "Frank" Siverd. Broad was born in Cornwall, England, in 1832 and immigrated to the United States when he was twenty. He first settled in New York City and then moved to Van Buren County, Michigan. He was known by his neighbors for his kindness and willingness to lend a hand. He soon became a naturalized citizen and moved to Lansing, where he married the recently widowed Charlotte Sherman in 1859.[19] Broad was employed by the state as a capitol porter when he enlisted at twenty-eight.[20] Frank Siverd moved to Lansing from his native state of Pennsylvania and soon became a favorite in the community. His popularity grew as his faithful correspondences, which he creatively entitled *Stray Leaves from Camp*, were published in the *Republican*. These letters detailed the adventures of the Third Regiment and Lansing's Company G. The paper reported Siverd's letters were so popular that many people subscribed for the sole purpose of reading his correspondence, and one young lady in Gratiot County walked four miles to pick up her paper.[21]

Company G was originally commanded by First Lieutenant Robert Jefferds, who was thirty-seven and a First Ward physician and surgeon, and forty-four-year-old Captain John Price. Captain Price, also a First Ward resident, worked in the agricultural tools supply business, making fanning mills used to separate grain from chaff. His intent from the very beginning, which he made known to the company, was to only accompany them through their training and not go to the field. This decision was made in large part due to family illness, his business responsibilities and, perhaps, his age. Lieutenant Jefferds was promoted to captain when, to the great consternation and disappointment of his men, Price resigned his commission in late July 1861, but not before the men under his command "saw the elephant" on the battlefield of Bull Run.[22]

The Lansing Company left the city in mid-May, and on the Sunday before their departure for Grand Rapids they gathered on the grounds of the state capitol, with a concourse of citizens to bid them farewell. Pocket Bibles were distributed to the men as "tears streamed down the faces of the soldiers and they pledged to be good boys, true to God and country."[23] The men were loaded onto lumber wagons for the trip to Bath to board the Amboy, Lansing and Traverse Bay Railroad, the nearest railroad to Lansing. This was thought to be one of the state's first known movements of troops

Historical marker at the site of Camp Anderson, Kent County Fairgrounds. *Photo courtesy of Ben Bever.*

by railroad.[24] The men rode the cars from Bath to Owosso to St. Johns and, eventually, Grand Rapids.

The companies of the Third Michigan Volunteer Infantry Regiment, some arriving after having walked over sixty miles, came from Lansing, Saranac, Grand Rapids, Lyons, Muskegon and Georgetown, and they were gathered at Cantonment Anderson.[25] Camp Anderson, named after Robert Anderson, the Union commander of Fort Sumter, was just south of Grand Rapids on the rather swampy, forty-acre site of the Kent County Agricultural Fairgrounds and racetrack.[26] Company G, which was originally designated as Company K, was mustered into state service on May 21, 1861, and took the federal oath of service on June 10.

Prior to their taking the oath, the entire regiment was examined by the regimental surgeon. A few were rejected due to "their lack of backbone." Upon examination, it was discovered that eighteen-year-old Edward Case of Lansing had a little finger unnaturally drawn down to the palm by a tendon contraction. The surgeon, who had an early war sense of duty, informed Case he could not be mustered in because the finger would "interfere with the manipulation of arms." When Case protested, stating "he could shoot just as well as any of them," the surgeon said he could have accepted him if the finger had been cut off, and "we have several in the regiment who have lost a finger"— an amputated digit apparently not being considered an interference. Case, seeing the precariousness of his situation, simply stated, "Well, then cut mine off," to which the surgeon replied, to the applause of the men, "You can pass." Case's dedication was an example of the fervent desire to serve held by these "fine, stalwart, brave men" of Lansing.[27]

In his first letter home to Lansing, "Stray Leaves from Camp No. 1," Frank Siverd described the conditions at Camp Anderson. To the delight of future historians, all of Frank's letters home were numbered. The grounds were enclosed by a high and tight wooden fence, with seven hundred men quartered in a two-story, 120-foot-long barrack, with up to five men per bunk. The bunks were furnished with straw ticks and one blanket per man; Siverd complimented the ladies of Lansing for furnishing Company G boys with very necessary extra blankets and quilts. The mess, or boarding hall, was 200 feet long with open sides. Three long tables seated the entire regiment of over one thousand men, and the bill of fare was "not exactly what you might expect at the Lansing House" hotel. Breakfast of coffee, sugar, beefsteak, boiled or fried potatoes and bread and butter was followed by dinner of "indescribable soup," boiled beef and potatoes, beans, bread and butter and water; supper consisted of tea, sugar, cold beef, more fried potatoes and, of course, bread and butter.[28]

The first week of June, the whole regiment received their gray uniforms. Some Union troops at the start of the war wore gray uniforms, which led to much confusion and many friendly fire casualties in their first engagement with the similarly gray-clad Confederates. To the dismay of Frank, and through no fault of theirs, the men from Lansing were shuffled about in order of company assignments from one of distinction, Company K, to one of lower standing, Company G. With the change of their company position, the men were also forced to give up their prized rifles, which they had brought with them from Lansing, and "though there was no swearing done, as that is against regulations, there was some very strong muttering."[29]

Prior to receiving their full uniforms, the men were marched to the nearby Grand River to bathe, which may have given the Lansing boys a sense of home. However, "six hundred men went out in the morning full of hilarity and joy and returned a few hours later in gloom and sorrow." While several hundred men were swimming, one of them was seized by cramps and sank in the twelve feet of water. According to Siverd, "Consternation seized the

Hand-embroidered presentation battle flag of the Third Michigan Volunteer Infantry Regiment carried by Color Sergeant Charles T. Foster. *Save the Flags*.

whole of them and they fled leaving him to his fate." Allen Shattuck, though some rods away, rushed to the site and unsuccessfully attempted to rescue the poor drowning man. He was the only person who made an effort. After a forty-minute search, the body was discovered, and Lieutenant Jefferds of the Rifles, who prior to his enlistment was a Lansing physician, unsuccessfully attempted to resuscitate him—yet one more example of the fine, stalwart, brave men from the capital city.[30]

That same week, the regiment received its battle flag. On June 4, a "vast assemblage of people"—at least four thousand—watched a delegation of thirty-four young women, representing the states in the Union, present the regiment with a "beautiful silken banner."

The flag is of the army size, six feet on the pike, and six feet six inches on the fly, of blue silk, with heavy yellow fringe, and on the front is elegantly embroidered in corn-colored silk, the arms of the United States and the words "Volunteers, Third Regiment, Mich." Upon the reverse appear the same arms and over and under them, the words "The Ladies of Grand Rapids to the Third Regiment Michigan Infantry," also embroidered. The work is of the most delicate and substantial kind. The embroidery is beautiful, the work of Maggie Ferguson, of our city, and the whole is attached to a pike ten feet long—it is a beauty and reflects more than ordinary credit upon the generous ladies who got it up.[31]

Maggie Ferguson would die of consumption soon after the regiment left for the field. Friends claimed she overexerted herself in order to finish the flag.

Carriages brought the girls to the camp, as well as a huge cavalcade of spectators, a brass band and a glee club. Six girls were selected to present the flag to the regiment. The six wore azure blue dresses with sashes of red and white and carried blue parasols with clusters of thirteen small gilt stars. The other girls wore red Zouave jackets and brown jockey hats trimmed with red, white and blue. As the band played and the glee club sang, the girls presented their flag. Then three cheers went up for the "Ladies of Grand Rapids" and three cheers for the flag. This flag, while cherished by the whole regiment, would come to hold special meaning to the boys of Lansing and to Charles T. Foster.

In the early morning hours of Thursday, June 13, as recorded by the *Grand Rapids Daily Eagle*, the Third Michigan marched through the streets of Grand Rapids from Camp Anderson to board the cars at the depot and entrain for war. They were led by the firemen of the city, the regimental band and the "colors of the regiment and their escort flying." The streets were thronged with citizens, family members and "women sobbing aloud," all coming to say their last good-byes. Among them were many new wives whose weddings had been moved up before their young husbands left for war, including the wife of Lieutenant James Ten Eyck of Lansing, who was married just four days earlier. The troops marched through the dense crowds and arrived at the depot, overflowing with people. The soldiers were covered with dust and looked grim. "Many a brown cheek showed the traces of tears....The scene was both singular and affecting." They then boarded two specially detailed trains to the waving of hats, hands and handkerchiefs and final farewells. As the crowd lost sight of the last car, people slowly and sadly dispersed "with lingering steps to darkened and lonely homes."[32]

The thirteen- and twelve-car baggage and coach trains, pulled by the locomotives Huron and Michigan, arrived at Detroit's Brush Street Depot at six o'clock that evening. The ladies of Detroit had spent the day in anticipation of the Third's arrival. They donated large quantities of food, including vegetables, meats, cakes, breads and mammoth hams, some beautifully decorated with cloves spelling out admonitions such as "Death to Traitors." In addition to tea, coffee and water, ales and lager were donated by several Detroit breweries. The "soldiers retreat" room was patriotically decorated with flags and banners, with the four-hundred-foot tables illuminated by eighteen gaslights that had been fitted up just for the occasion. Immediately after dinner at nine o'clock, the men embarked upon the propeller *Concord* and the steamer *Ocean*.[33] They sailed Lake Erie to Cleveland and from there rode the cars to their final destination, the encampments in the environs of the nation's capital, Washington, D.C. The Third Michigan and Company G had arrived at the seat of war.

Chapter 2

NO TOWN IN THE STATE
CAN EXCEL LANSING

Life in the City

The 1859 charter of the city of Lansing divided it into three city wards, and it was split into three geographic areas, those being Upper, Middle and Lower Town. Upper Town was the area west of the Grand River and Cedar Street and south of Main Street, commonly now known as REO Town. Middle Town consisted of the area between Ionia and Kalamazoo Streets, and Lower Town was the area now referred to as North Lansing or Old Town.[34] While all three areas included homes, hotels and businesses, Middle Town, where the capitol was located, although the last to develop, was considered by most to be the center of Lansing life and commerce. The city, having been incorporated in 1859, was very proud of the progress it had made since its founding, boasting of its "incomparable private residences, its large and commodious stores, its sidewalks and beautifully graded streets.…Ladies can now walk out morning, noon and night, without the slightest danger or risk of their lives from rickety sidewalks.…The most fastidious in dress can be suited…and the palate of the greatest epicurean can be gratified."[35] "Who says Lansing is not on the move?"[36]

Even with all this progress, the city still grappled with the embarrassment of "the running at large of hogs and horses.…No garden is safe";[37] runaway teams of horses, which often led to serious injuries or even fatalities; the occasional wandering cow; and sheep that were sometimes allowed to go at large.[38] The majority of street-grading work and sidewalk and road construction projects were halted due to the lack of labor and its high cost during the Civil War. This did not stop the citizens of Lansing from venting

Presbyterian Church, *Lansing Ing Co.*

Line drawing of the First Presbyterian Church of Lansing on the southwest corner of Washington Avenue and Genesee Street, 1859. *Library of Congress, Geography and Map Division.*

about holes in the streets not being properly repaired in a timely manner and, in the same breath, complaining about increased taxes to pay for such improvements, some matters being time immemorial. A great debate erupted in 1864 over whether or not the newly completed wooden bridge over the Grand River at Michigan Avenue should be covered. Opponents argued covering the bridge would increase the risk of fire, sleighs would not be able to cross the snow-barren span in the winter and the bridge would become a location for idlers and loafers—especially on Sundays.[39] Such were the weighty subjects facing the common council at the time.

According to the *Republican*, "Towns should be, and are, by all right-minded people measured by the number, size and style of their Churches…. Lansing is doing well in these respects."[40] The spiritual needs of the Lansing flock were well met by the First Methodist Episcopal Church on Wall Street and the Second Methodist, the Presbyterian and St. Paul's

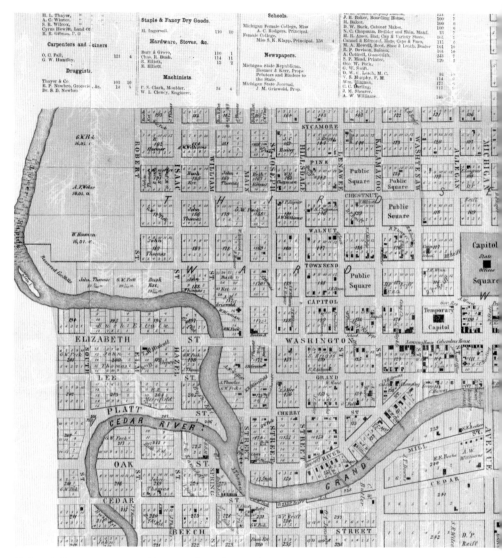

Geil and Company topographic map of the City of Lansing, 1859. *Geil, Harley and Siverd, Library of Congress, Geography and Map Division.*

Episcopal churches, all on Washington Avenue. The Baptists met on Capitol Avenue, the Free-Will Baptists on Kalamazoo Street and the Universalists on Grand Street. The German Lutherans and Methodists met at Kilborn and Saginaw Streets, respectively.[41] Services were also open to the public at the State Reform School just across the Grand River. Many of these congregations, temporarily lacking their own sanctuaries, were permitted to

hold their services in the chambers of the state capitol.[42] During the war, the city experienced a flurry of church construction with the Methodist church on Washington Avenue and the construction of a new, brick Universalist church on Grand Avenue. When the Universalist church opened in 1863, it was considered a credit to the city and included an organ of fine finish and excellent tone, it being the first one in the city.[43] The Catholic congregation lagged slightly behind its Protestant brethren in constructing a church. The foundations of a forty-by-sixty-foot Catholic church were laid near the start of the war around 1861, and with Catholics increasing in numbers in the vicinity, construction commenced again in 1864 with a church dedication in February 1865.[44]

Perhaps as a reflection of the ravages of war, and very personal loss, Lansing citizens appear to have embraced spirituality, clinging to faiths offering the promise of a hereafter and the hope of seeing loved ones again who had perished on the battlefield. "In regard to our city…no town in Michigan of the population of Lansing has done more in the way of building up churches…and it gives us pleasure, also to record the fact that the attendance upon the Sabbath upon these places of worship is exceedingly good."[45] Not missing the chance to evangelize, the *Republican* noted there were still a few vacant pews.

As important as the number of churches in measuring a community was the number and quality of its schools. The 1865 census of Lansing children between the ages of four and twenty years old reported their total number to be 1,118.[46] This census was conducted under the direction of the chairman of the committee on schools and was taken principally by Samuel Harris. First Lieutenant Harris, who fought with the Fifth Michigan Cavalry Regiment, had been severely wounded, losing the use of his left arm; he was taken prisoner, eventually paroled and came to Lansing to take a job working in Gillett's Jewelry Store. Harris was subsequently hired to conduct the census. School-age children attended three schools in the first, second and third city wards forty-two weeks a year, with the traditional holiday and summer breaks. The predominantly female teachers, including Misses Turner, King, Seymour, Parmalee and Greene, each made an annual average starting salary of $250.[47]

Recognizing the need for accommodations for legislators and Michiganders conducting business in the new capital city, numerous hotels were constructed, some of which included dining rooms. Among the first was the Seymour House, constructed in Lower Town (north Lansing) by early Lansing resident James Seymour around 1847 on the corner of Center and Franklin (East Grand River) Streets. The Lansing House was constructed the same year, on the corner of South Washington Avenue and East Washtenaw Street, but was consumed by fire in June 1861. In 1866, Lafayette Baker built a new hotel on the site that opened as the Lansing House and later became the Hotel Downey. Brevet General Baker, along with his cousin Lieutenant Luther Baker, played a leading role in the capture of Lincoln assassin John Wilkes Booth, and Lafayette used his substantial reward money to build the hotel. One of Lansing's first brick buildings was the Benton House Hotel

The Lansing House was constructed around 1847 on the corner of Washington Avenue and Washtenaw Street but was totally lost to fire the evening of June 2, 1861. *Library of Congress, Geography and Map Division.*

in Upper Town on the corner of South Washington and West Main Street. During the war, this hotel was converted to accommodate the Benton House Lansing Academy, which opened in the fall of 1863. Across from the old capitol on South Washington Avenue was the American, formerly the Eagle Hotel.[48] Other hotels appeared in the same period, including the Octagon and the Edgar Hotel on Washington Avenue—all constructed to meet the needs of the growing city.

The need for news and information was met by two newspapers published within the city: the *Lansing State Republican,* the voice of local Republicans, published on Michigan Avenue, and the competing and Democratic *Michigan State Journal*, with its printing press on Washington Avenue. The *State Republican* issued its first edition in April 1855 and was founded by prominent Detroit newspaperman Henry Barnes. After printing two editions, Barnes returned to Detroit and, in 1863, became the colonel of the First Michigan Colored Infantry Regiment. Several African American men from Lansing would see action with this regiment. Upon Barnes's departure, editing and publishing of the paper eventually passed to the firm of Fitch and Hosmer and then Hosmer and Kerr. John Kerr, who served as the second mayor of Lansing in 1860, continued as the publisher through the remainder of the war, while the job of editing changed hands frequently. The publisher of the paper was also normally the firm holding the lucrative contract for state printing. The four-page, seven-column paper was published every Wednesday and cost subscribers one dollar per year until 1864, when the price was doubled and the number of columns was expanded to eight.[49] The forerunner to the *Michigan State Journal* was first published in 1848, but with the ranks of citizens aligning themselves with the Republican Party increasing, subscriptions to the paper subsided, as did advertisements, and it was forced to halt publication in November 1861. It was resurrected in May 1863, ceased publishing again in March 1865 and began publication again one year later as the *Lansing Democrat*.

The question arises: How did the citizens of Lansing make their living during the war? They worked at jobs not unlike the occupations of today, including farming. Lansing was situated in "the center of a fine farming district," with an abundance of grain and sheep farmers. In 1863, Lansing

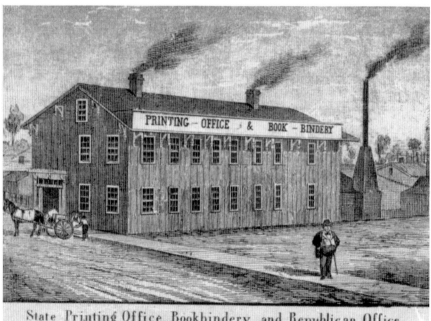

The printing office of the *Lansing State Republican* on Michigan Avenue. The paper was published every Wednesday by Rufus Hosmer and John Kerr. *Library of Congress, Geography and Map Division.*

shipped over two hundred thousand pounds of locally produced wool, and its two flouring mills turned out ten thousand barrels of flour.

The state government offered positions for men working as clerks and government employees, although many of these were seasonal, based on the part-time Michigan legislature then convening only for the first few months of the year, under the leadership of the Republican governor Austin Blair. Governor Blair and the legislature, along with the newly appointed and very capable adjutant general, John Robertson, faced the daunting challenge of outfitting the newly formed Michigan regiments—a challenge well met with the assistance of many Lansing men who were employed by the state, many of whom would also see service in the war.

The newly created Michigan Reform School also employed several citizens. "The number of hands they employed…made a considerable addition to the business interests of the city."[50] The 1863 *State Gazetteer* reported that in Lansing there were three tanneries, three sawmills, two sash and blind shops, three iron foundries and machine shops, two printing offices, several brickyards and a large number of mechanic shops.[51] Men were also employed in the manufacture of chairs, furniture and coffins, such as those sold by Daniel Buck in his Middle Town furniture store. Lansing was home to the cottage industry production of shoes, boots and leather accessories, including harnesses and equipment for the farm. Carpenters were likewise making their living building homes and dozens of stores and businesses, offering practically everything citizens needed or desired, as well as employment opportunities.

Ladies could purchase dresses and hats at Miss Barret's, Miss Edgerly's, Miss McGeorge's, Miss Parment's, Miss Warner's or Mr. Beebe's millineries. Clothing for men and children and sundry necessary household goods were offered by numerous dry goods stores, including Peck and Merrifield, Simon's, Turner's, Mead's, Ingersoll's and Hinman's, Englehardt's, Coryell and Jenison or Bailey's. While having your watch repaired at Hinman's Jewelry, men could buy their tobacco products at Hinckley's Tobacco and medicines at Thayer's Drugstore and then wander over to Luther Jameison's or Andrew Bertch's meat markets. Those needing wagons or carriages could find them at P.G. Sprang's shop at the foot of Washtenaw Street, along with the services of numerous liveries and stables. Those desiring to have their likeness taken could venture over to the portrait studios of Cheney and Baker or Phil Engelhardt's in Middle Town. "We presume no one will allow their friends to go to the war without exchanging pictures with them before they go.…Many of them we may never see again."[52]

BUSINESS DIRECTORY.

Attorneys and Counsellors at Law. (Block / Lot)
J. W. & E. Longyear, 100 6
J. G. & T. J. Ramsdell, 114 9
D. C. Wiley, 114 9
Armstrong, G. A. 114 7
K. C. Dart, 100 6
Wm. H. Chapman, 111 14
Wm. H. Pinckney, State Off.
C. W. Butler, 128 2

Architects and Builders.
M. Elder, 244 5
J. J. Jeffres,

Builders.
C. C. Dodge,
S. R. Greene, 130 4
P. C. Ayers, 132 2
G. H. Gassemere, 11 4
H. L. Olcott, 27 5
W. Ward, 151 12
J. H. Winn, 116 3

Blacksmiths.
S. Lansing,
J. Newson & W M 14 2
Jacob Berner, 12 1

Bricklayers, Masons, and Carpenters.
P. Sopry, 18 2
A. H. Marsh,

Clerks.
S. D. Bingham, Aud. Gen. Office
D. W. Bagley, "
W. C. Bennett, "
I. McCravath, "
J. S. Cressey, "
C. W. Church, "
A. V Dearin, "
O. A. Gunison, "
Jos. Mills, "
H. L. Thayer, "
A. C. Winter, "
S. R. Wilcox, "
Cyrus Hewitt, Land Of
R. R. Gibson, P. O.

Carpenters and Joiners.
O. C. Fall, 131 4
G. W. Huntley,

Druggists.
Thayer & Co. 101 10
E. P. Newbro, Grocerie, &c. 14 5
Dr. S. D. Newbro

Editors.
R. Hosmer, Republican.
J. M. Griswold, Journal

Farmers.
W. F. Davis,
W. S. Calkins.
O. F. Camp.

Grocery and Provision Dealers.
A. B. Bagley, 111 5
Chas. Wibit, 14 5
A Englehardt, 5 12

Hotels.
Lansing House, M. P. Marvin, 129 12
Columbus House, J. G. Darling, 114 10
Seymour House, H. Angel, 13 2

Justices of the Peace.
C. Havens, 114 7
A. Ward, 116 6

Livery Stables.
F. La Rue, 126 1
H. Angel, 13 2

MERCHANTS.

Dry Goods, Groceries, &c.
Jno. Thomas & Co. 116 10
Cowles, F. M. 116 1
E. R. Merrifield, 116 10
S. Briggs, 114 9
A. F. Weller, 116 10
H. B. Smith, 14 5
D. W. Van Auken, 12 2
J. Turner, 6 7
Mead & Robson, 6 8

Staple & Fancy Dry Goods.
H. Ingersoll, 116 10

Hardware, Stoves, &c.
Burr & Grove, 116 1
Chas. R. Bush, 114 11
R. Elliott, 13 2
E. Elliott.

Machinists.
P. S. Clark, Moulder, 34 4
W. L. Clency, Engineer.

Millers and Millwrights.
Alex. Cline,
Thomas Shively
R. W. Burdick, 13 2

Ministers of the Gospel.
Rev. C. S. Armstrong, Pastor of Presbyterian Church, 53 2
" J. Somerville, Chap. State Ref. School.
" A. Bower, Past. U. B. Ch.
C. W. Knickerbacker, Pastor of Universalist Church, 112 1

Physicians and Surgeons.
H. B. Shank, 101 7
C. O. Scoot,
I. H. Bartholomew, 141 12
Hull, J. B. 69 1
H. T. Hawley, Homeopathic. 95 2
E. Price, M. D. 114 7
J. S. Wood, 56
J. Phillips, 22
O. B. Webster, 4 2
P. W. Gillson, M. D. Botanic. 135 9

Land and Tax Agents.
Turner & Case, 6 7
Woodhouse & Butler, 128 2
S. S. Coryell,
L. D. Preston, Surveyor, 33 1

Land Brokers.
D. P. Reiff,
W. H. Chapman, 111 14

Saddle, Harness and Trunk Manufacturers.
Camuel & Edmonds, 111 6
J. Somerville, 12 1

Schools.
Michigan Female College, Miss A. C. Rodgers, Principal.
Female College,
Miss S. K. Klapp, Principal. 136 4

Newspapers.
Michigan State Republican, Hosmer & Kerr, Props
Printers and Binders to the State.
Michigan State Journal, J. M. Griswold, Prop.

Merchant Tailors and Clothiers.
M. L. Miller,
J. W. Downs.

Tailors.
Westcott, T. W., Draper
Westcott, D
Dixon, J. B.

State Officers.
Moses Wisner, Governor.
E. B. Fairfield, Lieut. Gov
N. G. Isbell, Secretary of State
E. A. Thompson, Dep. Sec. of State
John McKinney, Treasurer.
Theo. Hunter, Dep. "
D. L. Case, Auditor General.
Ezra Jones, Dep. "
J. M. Howard, Attorney General
J. M. Gregory, Sup. Pub. Inst'n.
J. W. Sanborn, Com. Land Office
H. B. Treadwell, Dep. "
J. E. Tenney, Librarian

Miscellaneous.
J. C. Bailey & Co., Bankers.
J. R. Williams, Pres. St. Agr'l. College
I. Jillett, Jr., Watchmaker & Jeweller,
Alvin Upson, Miss. A. S. S.
A. J. Viele, City Book Store.
J. R. Price, Fanning Mill Manufacturer.
J. Tompkins & Co., Furnace & Machine Shops.
R. Turner, Plow-wooder.
J. S. Tooker, Moulder.
E. Partaulee, Sash & Blind Manufacturer and Wool Carder,
M. A. Thayer, Lumber Dealer.
J. I. Mead, Dealer in Hides & Leather,
Geo. Beale, Brickmaker.
F. Weinman, Brewery.
L. C. Damon, Tinman,
Dr. S. D. Newbro, Phonographist and General Business Agent.
Tim Wilson, Barber and Hair Dresser.
H. Wilcox, House, Sign & Orn'l Painter.
H. H. Dunks, Deputy Sheriff.
J. B. Baker, Boarding House,
H. Baker,
D. W. Buck, Cabinet Maker.
N. C. Chapman, Builder and Shin. Manf.
H. B. Ames, Hat, Cap & Variety Store.
Camuel & Edmond, Hats, Caps & Furs.
M. A. Howell, Boot, Shoe & Leath. Dealer
E. P. Davison, Saloon.
A. Cottrell, Gunsmith,
S. P. Mead, Printer,
Geo W. Peck,
G. W. Swift.
D. W. C. Leach, M. C.
V. S. Murphy, P. M.
Wm. Hinman,
C. C. Darling,
J. M. Shearer,
A. W. Williams.

Above: Lansing City Directory, 1859, published with topographic map of the City of Lansing, 1859. *Geil, Harley and Siverd, Library of Congress, Geography and Map Division.*

Opposite: The Cowles block in Middle Town, including the businesses of Charles S. Hunt and F.M. Cowles. *Library of Congress, Geography and Map Division.*

Banking needs were met at the Middle Town bank of J.C. Bailey and Company, while medical needs were satisfied at the offices of John Bacon, Ira Bartholomew, Henry Hawley, Joseph Hull, Charles Jeffries, Eleazer Price or H.B. Shank, many of whom practiced homeopathic medicine and some of whom would see service as medical officers in the war. Citizens requiring legal advice and services could seek out Edmund Burtch, Rollin Dart, Stephen Bingham, Ephraim and John Longyear or Delos Wiley. Those seeking dental relief could find it in the offices of Stacy A. Morrison or J.L. Lanterman, both in Middle Town, with Lanterman specializing in the mounting of teeth in gold or silver. A haircut or shave could be had at the barbershops of Timothy Wilson, Charles Martin and Benjamin Cooper

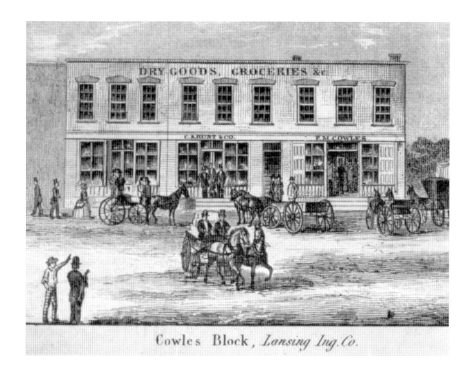

Cowles Block, *Lansing Ing.Co.*

in Middle Town. These barbers were part of the small African American community in Lansing, which hovered around thirty citizens.[53]

The capital city also served as the center of entertainment, which included speeches by traveling dignitaries, sermons delivered by itinerant ministers, prestidigitators, rope walkers, informative presentations by visiting lecturers, musical presentations, vocal recitals and theatrical productions, many of which took place in the chambers of the capitol. There were also several smaller entertainment venues, which included Mead's Hall, Dodge's Hall and, in 1864, the newly constructed Chapman/Capital Hall in the capitol block on Washington Avenue. The fine brick building was constructed by Mayor William Chapman and hosted traveling entertainers including ventriloquist Professor De Castro and Whitney the Magician, who was a "celebrated master of the science of necromancy, mysticism and wonder"[54]— necromancy being the practice of black magic and communication with the dead. Merchants Ingersoll and Hinman also operated a small hall above their newly constructed brick store in Middle Town, where the Metropolitan Theater Troupe performed to great acclaim. Most of these "halls" were simply the upper floors of storefronts, which in true "shotgun building" fashion were narrow and long and only able to accommodate small audiences. The halls frequently served as meeting spaces for local fraternal organizations, such as the three Masonic Lodges that were very active in Lansing during the war, the Odd Fellows or the several Firemen's Associations, which likewise supplied many military volunteers.

The winter months found citizens indulging in skating and sleigh races on the Grand River; the *Republican* frequently reported on the favorable conditions for both. "Good sleighing is 'lying loose.'...Nothing is more pleasant than a sleigh-ride with spirited horses and plenty of *belles*. We like it best when the weather is sufficiently cold to require two to keep one shawl."[55] A Lansing citizen, years later, proclaimed he could "remember when sleighing used to be an institution in this town."[56] New Year's Day found the river "thronged with sleighs, cutters, jumpers, men and boys."[57] A mile-long course had been laid out on the ice and in "the unexpected absence of the reporters from the New York Sporting Press," [58] the *Republican* gave the minutes of the race.

In the last year of the war, the new craze of baseball hit the capital city with the formation of a league and Lansing fielding a fine team of strikers playing for the Capital Club. There were frequent home runs as a result of the ball being lost in the uncut outfield grass. Croquet was likewise gaining in popularity. Lansing was home to several billiards rooms, but "these are looked upon by most of the citizens as novelties unworthy of patronage, by those having an earnest respect for themselves and the good of society."[59] We got trouble, and that starts with *T* and rhymes with *P* and stands for *pool*, right here in Lansing city, with very little doubt what playing pool leads to.

In 1855, the Michigan legislature passed an "iron clad" law to "prevent the Manufacture and Sale of Spirituous or Intoxicating Liquors,"[60] with an exception for liquor for medicinal purposes, sold by bonded druggists. Enforcement of the law, however, was left to individual municipalities, and the law was applied by degrees based largely on local opinions of temperance. There was also the question of whether wine, ciders and beer were intoxicating, and this led to a gray area in enforcement. In defiance or ignorance of the state prohibition law passed within the chambers of the capitol in their very own city, numerous saloons and several breweries called Lansing home, including the Middle Town saloons of Charles Babo, Stanley Briggs, Daniels and Williams and Lehmann's, as well as the Schoettle and Weinman breweries.[61] Lehmann's, located in the same block as the capitol, boasted it had pure Buffalo Lager Beer and Detroit Ale on draught and advertised as such in the pages of the *Republican*. Despite the efforts of many citizens and sermons advocating temperance from the pulpits of Lansing

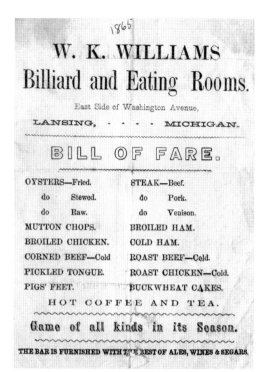

Left: Bill of fare from W.K. Williams Billiard and Eating Rooms, east side of Washington Avenue. *Collection of Craig Whitford.*

Right: Advertisement for Dan Rice's Great Show, *State Republican*, July 23, 1862. *https://www. newspapers.com/image/326045459/.*

churches, by 1865, the claim was made that the city was home to no fewer than twenty saloons.[62]

In the midst of war, Lansing citizens attempted to cling to normalcy; they tended their gardens, with the size and quantity of their produce compared in the *Republican* and the editors encouraging their readers to supply them with samples. They cared for their children, went to work, attended church services and sought relief from the daily stress of the conflict gripping the nation through occasional entertainment. At least six major circuses visited Lansing from 1860 to 1865, including the R. Sands Gigantic Combination Circus in 1860, Robinson and Lake's Menagerie in 1861, Dan Rice's Great Show in 1862, with an encore performance in 1865, and the Ocean Circus in the fall of 1864. Exemplifying the palpable incongruence of peace and war, the home front versus the front lines, in the same May 25, 1864 edition of the *Republican* that listed the fearful and growing casualties of

General Grant's Overland Campaign—including a firsthand account of the butchery of battle by Lansing native Edward Flower—was an advertisement for Howe's Great European Circus. The circus audience was entertained by the "cage of lions" while many boys from Lansing were fighting to the death like just so many caged animals on the Virginia battlefields of the Wilderness and Spotsylvania.

Chapter 3

The Brave Boys Go

Company G Enters the Fray

T he Third Michigan and Lansing-based Company G arrived in Washington, D.C., on Sunday, June 16, 1861, and encamped at Georgetown Heights between the First and Second Michigan Infantry Regiments, about eight miles from Alexandria, Virginia. The arriving western troops gave some relief to the citizens of D.C., the city having been virtually unprotected from Confederate attack. Frank Siverd reported "a welcome met us everywhere....All were in good spirits....The city is not as well guarded as we were led to think and a capture by surprise would I think not be impossible."[63] The soldiers received their new U.S. uniforms of blue blouses, pants and caps. When not standing guard, the men of Company G were able to reacquaint themselves with friends from Lansing who were serving in the First and Second Regiments, including Major Williams of the Second, their former commander of the Rifles, and the Reverend Edward Meyer, rector of St. Paul's Episcopal Church in Lansing, who was serving as chaplain for the First Michigan. "In the evening a hundred bonfires lighted up the banks and hills of the Potomac for miles; each camp was a blaze of light; it was a sight."[64] The regiment was also reviewed by President Lincoln and Secretary of State Seward. The president complimented the regiment "for the fine appearance of the men."[65]

A natural phenomenon made nightly visits to Union and Confederate soldiers encamped across North America in the early summer months of 1861. What would come to be commonly known as the "war comet" appeared on clear nights for almost three months starting in late June. According to

Siverd, "The comet which made its appearance unheralded and without ceremony is the theme of conversation in each little knot of soldiers, and it is amusing as well as edifying to hear the various Philosophical disquisitions on its origin, destination and what it portends."[66] The comet, which has been classified by astronomers as being among the eight greatest comets of the nineteenth century, conjured up mixed emotions among the men. Some were certain it portended upcoming defeat, others that it predicted imminent victory on the battlefield, questions soon to be answered along the quietly flowing stream of Bull Run near the town of Manassas, Virginia.

The Third Michigan spent the days leading up to the First Battle of Bull Run (also known as the Battle of Manassas) marching from D.C. with periodic encounters between men on picket duty, probing the defenses of the enemy. The Confederates tended to refer to battles by the place names of towns or villages near the battle, while Northern troops referred to them by the names of nearby bodies of water. Portions of the Third Michigan engaged the Confederate forces for the first time on July 18 at Blackburn's Ford.[67] Then, on Sunday, July 21, 1861, the massed Confederate and Union armies clashed at the First Battle of Bull Run, thirty miles southwest of Washington, D.C. The Third was on the extreme flank of the Union line, and after the Union defeat, they covered the retreat. According to Siverd, they were "the last off the field….We have surely passed through a fiery furnace and most of us have come out unscathed."[68] Siverd had the uncanny good fortune of meeting his three brothers on the battlefield, all serving with Pennsylvania regiments. It had been three years since their last parting.[69] Allen Shattuck was posted on picket duty, and when he came in, he realized the regiment and army had begun the retreat and the regimental colors had been accidently left behind. At great risk to his own life, Shattuck, along with several other men, took down the flag and caught up with the regiment.[70]

During the reorganization of the defeated and disheartened Army of the Potomac after Bull Run, the Third encamped at Hunter's Place near Arlington, Virginia, within sight of rebel fortifications. They were engaged in creating clearings out of the woods, called "slashings," to increase the effectiveness and range of the Union artillery. The men attempted to battle the "unbearable heat" in the pea-green waters of the Potomac and occupied a "splendid camping ground." Many of the men were in the hospital as a result of illness, and many would succumb to disease that summer and fall, including William Choates, James Dalton and Ira Turner, all from Lansing. With the resignation of Captain Price, Lieutenant Jefferds was promoted to captain and made a short visit to Lansing to comfort his ailing wife. Allen

Shattuck's father, who was stationed nearby with the U.S. Sharpshooters, visited the regiment, and father and son were briefly reunited for the first time since their enlistments in Lansing the previous spring. Allen was promoted to eighth corporal in recognition of his bravery at Bull Run in retrieving the regimental colors. "If the same bearers and guard are to be retained, the ladies of Grand Rapids need never fear that the colors…will ever be taken by the rebels."[71] The colors of the Third were flown over Union Fort Richardson and were "flung to the breeze from the highest point of the heights…greeted by three times three.…The Lansing boys claim the credit of saving them."[72]

Perhaps feeling nostalgic at missing the fall deer-hunting season in Michigan, which had been instituted in 1859, in a September 6 letter home, Siverd compared picket duty on the outposts to still-hunting for deer in Michigan, with one major difference: "While you are anxiously watching for the appearance of your own game, you may yourself be bagged, and your head carried off as a trophy by some rebel sharpshooter." He also compared army scouts to Michigan squirrel hunters and assured the readers of the *Republican*, "The Michigan 3d will not disgrace the Peninsular State, nor Co. G the Capital thereof."[73]

Siverd reported that the boys attended their first divine service since leaving Lansing, at Christs Church in Alexandria, Virginia. The brick church was seven miles from Mount Vernon, and George Washington had been a regular worshipper there. "It seems to me that the spirit of the Great Patriot must have arisen and rebuked the treason"[74] that has been recently preached here, Siverd wrote. On a march through Alexandria, they passed an old slave pen marked by the sign "Smith and Brothers, Dealers in Slaves." The sign had been whitewashed by Union troops, but Siverd noted, "Like many efforts to whitewash the peculiar institution, the blood upon the hand would not stay covered."[75] Siverd and several Company G men spent two days on a reconnaissance mission with Major Williams of the Second Michigan. During this scouting mission, they saw the direct effect of the war in the barren countryside. Plantations, once productive, lay neglected and abandoned, with the majority of the owners and farmhands now within the ranks of the Confederate armies. The countryside, according to Siverd, lay wasted due to the "polluting presence of slavery and its twin sister, treason.…Slavery battled long with nature, but succumbed at last.…War with its terrible scourge has been here and left an indelible mark."[76]

In November, the regiment unofficially celebrated Thanksgiving, which would not be officially declared a national holiday until 1863, when

President Lincoln proclaimed it a holiday in commemoration of the Union victory at the Battle of Gettysburg. Work details were cancelled, and the men reminisced about past Thanksgivings at home: church services, afternoon dinners of turkey and plum pudding and evening parties. The soldiers had a special oyster dinner while the officers and noncommissioned officers partook of the traditional turkey dinner, cooked by a local contraband, who had recently fled his master's nearby plantation with the bird in tow.[77]

Company G went into winter quarters with ten to thirteen men in specially altered Sibley tents. Soldiers typically set up substantial "barracks" during the winter months and made them so appealing as to be reluctant to vacate them for spring campaigning. The men would quite often build elevated wooden bases, bunks and fireplaces, using old, mud-lined barrels as chimneys. According to Siverd, the men of Lansing went so far as to name their shelters: "The Eagles Nest"; "The Lions Lair," complete with brick floor; "The Tigers Den," which was the envy even of the officers; "The Lansing Rangers"; and "The Lansing House," which was a tribute to the Lansing Hotel and built with hewn logs for sides and roof. The men, "with a little work and ingenuity make themselves quite comfortable even when surrounded with Virginia mud." During the winter lull in fighting, they were issued Austrian rifles, and several men, including Homer Thayer, were sent back to Lansing on a recruiting mission.[78]

On March 13, 1862, the men left the comfort of their winter shelters and were marched to Fort Lyon overlooking Alexandria, where they spent three miserable days and nights, unprotected and exposed to severe storms that assumed the proportions of a gale, while waiting to board transport ships. On the seventeenth, they boarded the steamer *John Brooks* on the Potomac. The flotilla of eleven transports and numerous towed barges swung into line and left Alexandria, passed Mount Vernon and rendezvoused with other transports on the Upper Potomac. Siverd said the view from the deck of the steamer "was full of beauty. It was a beautiful moonlit night; the waters were as placid as an inland lake…the bosom of the Potomac, here several miles wide, tipping the ripples in the gaudy, colors of the rainbow."[79] They sailed to the Chesapeake Bay and then Fortress Monroe and Hampton, Virginia, where they disembarked. At Hampton, the boys encamped for several days and augmented their scanty rations by digging for oysters along the shore. "It was quite amusing to see several hundred men, up to their knees in mud and water delving after shell-fish. We lived on the fat of the land, or rather of the water, for a few days."[80] The regiment then commenced its march toward Yorktown and the numerous battles of the Peninsula Campaign.

The Peninsula Campaign was the brainchild of Union general George B. McClellan and was an attempt to capture the Confederate capital of Richmond by moving up the peninsula between the James and York Rivers. At Yorktown, the Union and Confederate armies built up their defenses, and for two weeks the Union army attempted to soften the Confederate defenses in preparation for a full-scale attack. This attack was, however, preempted by the Confederate withdrawal to the entrenchments of Williamsburg, farther up the peninsula. In passing through the abandoned Confederate works at Yorktown, the Union soldiers had their first experience with land mines or, as Siverd referred to them, "the hell devised torpedo or infernal machines, which were scattered or buried in various places.…A number of our men were killed or wounded by these machines."[81] The use of "weapons that wait" posed serious ethical questions both then and now, and many historians believe their use in the American Civil War helped to establish them as brutal and indiscriminate conveyors of death.

On May 21, 1862, the *Republican* published what would be Eli "Frank" Siverd's last letter home, postmarked Williamsburg, Virginia. In his letter, Frank described the vicious fighting on May 5 and "the horrors of the battle-field" of Williamsburg. In a heavy downpour, the men were soaked to the skin and rushed along to the front line, first on the quick, on the double quick and then on the run. By one o'clock in the afternoon, they reached the line; their knapsacks were unslung and rifles examined to ensure the falling rain had not made them inoperable. Then a final double-quick dash through the mud to where the Michigan Second and Fifth Regiments were engaged in hand-to-hand combat. The regimental colors that day were carried by Sergeant Charles T. Foster. The color sergeant of the regiment had "given out," and the major rode to the front of the regiment and asked, "Who of the sergeants will volunteer to carry the colors through this fight?" After a few long moments, with no one else seeming to want to take on the predictably deadly assignment, Foster stepped forward and volunteered to carry the colors.[82]

While being a color-bearer during the Civil War was an incredible honor, it was also recognized as a virtual sentence of death. The regiments rallied around the flags, and they became the focal point of combat, as the enemy recognized the surest way to confuse and dishearten the opposing force was to kill the man who was carrying the flag. As a result, amazing, almost unfathomable acts of bravery took place around the colors. Foster carried the colors through the carnage of the Battle of Williamsburg "in a most gallant manner."[83] "Side by side lay friend and foe, their eyes glazed in death—here is one cut to pieces with a shell, another transfixed with a bayonet, but a great majority were shot in the breast or head."[84]

The day after the battle, Charles wrote a letter to his family in Lansing. "When the Major called for volunteers and none of the sergeants seemingly to want to take the responsible and dangerous position I felt it was my duty to do so, for someone must do it, and if none would volunteer, a detail would have to be made, and the lot might fall on one who had a wife and children at home, or a dependent father or mother, and could not be spared, whereas, I was single and free, and would not be missed if I should be killed."[85] Foster would never learn of the anguish generated and the tears shed by his mother upon reading that line, to think her eldest son thought he would not be missed if he perished upon the field of battle.

After Williamsburg, the Confederate forces again withdrew to their last line of defense before the gates of Richmond. The Union lines were so close to the city that the soldiers recorded hearing the church bells of the Confederate capital. Then, on May 31, in a surprising turn of events, the Confederates attacked at Seven Pines or Fair Oaks, Virginia, just south of the Chickahominy River. The fighting was brutal, and the Third Michigan was in the whirlwind of combat. The color-bearer unable or perhaps unwilling to fulfill his obligation, Sergeant Foster stepped forward and volunteered once again for the dangerous duty. Foster bore the colors "through charge after charge and always with the flag well to the front, and until he was stricken by a Minnie ball through the neck. He went down— but not the flag—for here again we see a manifestation of his keen sense of duty to keep the flag aloft—for as he fell, he drove the flag staff into the ground; still grasping the staff with both hands he called to his comrades, 'Don't let the colors go down.'"[86] It was necessary to pry each of his fingers from the staff in order to retrieve the colors.

In a letter to his sister Lydia, just a few months after his son died, Theodore wrote: "We found as soon as our Charles was departed, that we were even more deeply attached to him than we supposed" and that he knew they would most likely never be able to bring his body home to Lansing.[87] "The tears often start as we think of one who lies buried in his blood-soaked clothes far away, but when we see the comrades who stood by his side come home crippled and wounded, to suffer for many years, we bless God that he died immediately, without pain or misery."[88] After receiving word that his son, Quentin, had been killed in an aerial dogfight over the battlefields of France during World War I, President Theodore Roosevelt wrote, "To feel that one has inspired a boy to conduct that has resulted in his death, has a pretty serious side for a father."[89] A memorial marker for Charles lies in Lansing's Mount Hope Cemetery in the Foster family plot. Charles's name adorns the Michigan State University alumni chapel, among the first of many Spartans to die for flag and country. At the end of the war, the Grand Army of the Republic post in Lansing was named after Charles. Walking past his home on Chestnut Street, most casual pedestrians—and perhaps even the current owners—are unaware that, so many years ago, a true American hero lived there, lying at rest in his bedroom, contemplating his promising future, before being thrown into the madness and utter brutality that is all war.

Just a few moments after Charles Foster was killed, Eli "Frank" Siverd was also mortally wounded. When word of his death reached the capital, the *Republican* eulogized Siverd: "Truly a friend has fallen….He was a young man of great intelligence; of high toned religious sentiment…the embodiment of virtuous principles….We can now hear his hearty laugh… feel the warm shake of the hand, while we remember his ready wit and kindly greeting….His life blood has been poured freely out as a sacrifice to this unholy war."[90] Also printed was a thank-you note from Elizabeth Siverd, of Gap, Pennsylvania, gratefully acknowledging the kindness of the citizens of her son's adopted home and thanking Mr. and Mrs. Thayer for sharing the particulars of her son's death as conveyed to them by their son, Homer.

Before his death, Frank requested that Homer continue the correspondence to Lansing, and in his first letter to the paper, dated June 3, Sergeant Thayer had the sad duty of reporting the casualties of the Third Regiment and Company G. At the Battle of Fair Oaks, 1 officer and 25 men were killed, 8 officers and 104 men were wounded and 27 men were listed as missing in action. "The loss of our Lansing company is severe and comprises some of the best men of the company."[91] Charles Foster was the first to fall, and E.F. Siverd was soon after mortally wounded, they being a part of the 11,200 total Union and Confederate casualties. "I would gladly speak of the merits of each of our company who are dead, had I the ability of doing as they deserve, they were beloved by all…and fought with a determination seldom equaled….I earnestly hope it may not be my duty to again report losses such as these….I will try to keep your readers informed….I am well aware they will miss 'Stray Leaves from Camp' and with us, mourn the loss of their author."[92]

In the Seven Pines National Cemetery in Henrico County, Virginia, eight miles southeast of Richmond, lie the disinterred and reburied remains of many of the fallen from the Battle of Fair Oaks. The 1.9 acres of grassy lawn contain the graves of almost 1,300 Union soldiers, only 150 of them identified. In plot 152 lie Sergeant E.F. Siverd and Sergeant Charles T. Foster, sharing in death the close bond they shared in life at home in Lansing, Michigan.[93]

Another casualty of Fair Oaks was Lansing's John Broad. Broad was called into the line and was barely there two minutes before he was hit. He was shot through the left arm; the bones shattered, and a rifle ball passed under his left eye and through the bridge of his nose and lodged behind his right eye. He was dragged behind some stumps by a comrade and was officially listed as dead, with the certificate witnessed by his friend Allen Shattuck. His body lay there until someone came by and threw him up on a brush pile so that the burial detail could find him. The next evening, Broad "came back to life" and was awakened by the sound of voices—"Is the poor devil dead?" "Wonder whose old carcass that is?"—leaving him to suffer in the hot sun, exposed to swarms of flies and mosquitoes. Finally, a comrade from Lansing realized Broad was in fact not dead and got him some much-needed water, and he came to on Wednesday. He had been wounded and "killed" the previous Saturday.

Homer Thayer enlisted with Company G in Lansing in 1861 and mustered out of the service in 1867 as a brevet major of U.S. Volunteers. *Collection of Lille Foster.*

The army doctors did not give Broad much chance of survival, so they provided only limited care to him. His desire to live, however, was tenacious, and he started to mend. Although he was able to regain part of his sight after five months, the bullet remained lodged behind his right eye the rest of his life and gave him almost constant pain. After his recuperation, Broad more than qualified for the Invalid Corps, but he refused and demanded to be sent back to his regiment. He fought with distinction for another year until being discharged in 1864. The *Republican,* while reporting on soldiers who had recently received the Medal of Honor, which was first awarded during the Civil War, lamented that Broad was not a recipient: "Not a man who received the Medals of Honor recently…was more justly deserving of the reward than John Broad, from this city. May he live long to wear the laurels which he has earned."[94] And live long he did. Broad was well known and loved throughout Lansing; he worked as a porter in the capitol and was very active in the Charles T. Foster Post of the Grand Army of the

Republic. Broad died in September 1915 and was buried in Lansing's Mt. Hope Cemetery. In a last interview in 1912, Broad said, "I'll probably stay dead until all of those 'honest' or real dead ones back in the Fair Oaks swamp are resurrected and the order given to fall in."[95]

There were many other Lansing casualties at Fair Oaks. David Webb, who had enlisted at eighteen and was an apprentice to Lansing cabinetmaker Daniel Buck, was wounded and eventually discharged as a result of his injuries. Also wounded were Henry Mange, a farmer from Clinton County who had enlisted in Lansing, and Lawrence Croy, a First Ward day laborer, who had his left leg fractured and was also eventually discharged as a result of the injury. When he died in 1908, his death certificate listed his wartime injury and disability as having contributed to his death. Charles Schasberger was also killed.

After the Battle of Fair Oaks, the armies clashed again in late June in a series of battles known as the Seven Days. For one solid week, the Union and Confederate soldiers attacked and counterattacked, and the Third was engaged at Savage Station, Peach Orchard, Glendale, White Oak Swamp and Malvern Hill. Unable to take Richmond, General McClellan withdrew from the Peninsula, and the Union army made its way back to D.C.

The Third was engaged that fall in the Second Battle of Bull Run in August, where Sergeant George Ellis was mortally wounded and twenty-year old Corporal William Hogan was killed. Ellis was a First Ward teamster and had two brothers fighting with Lansing-based Company B, of the Second U.S. Sharpshooters Regiment, one of whom would die at the infamous Confederate prison at Andersonville. In September, the regiment fought at Chantilly and Fredericksburg on December 13, 1862.

Lieutenant Joseph Mason, who was from DeWitt but was well known in Lansing, was sent home that fall to recruit for Company G, in an attempt to fill its depleted ranks, setting up his recruiting office in the Eagle Hotel. Company G "was the first Company which left this city for the seat of war, and it has been an honor to our county. An opportunity is now offered to such as feel disposed to enlist under tried and experienced officers, and in a regiment, which has reaped glorious honors on the field of battle."[96] Mason was soon promoted to captain and left for the front, leaving the recruiting duties to another Company G soldier, Joseph Stevens, who was also from Lansing. Among the new recruits was Michael Kane of Lansing. Kane was born in Canada, but when he was eight, his family immigrated to the United States, came to Lansing and witnessed "Lansing grow from a small village to the thriving city that it is today."[97] Four months after his recruitment, Kane was wounded at the Battle of Fredericksburg,[98] and he would be wounded again in 1864 at the Battle of Cold Harbor.[99]

The Third went into winter quarters after the Battle of Fredericksburg, where it encamped until April 28, 1863, when it again crossed the Rappahannock River and was engaged at the Battle of Chancellorsville from April 30 to May 6. In yet another letter home, Homer Thayer wrote, "The fighting was desperate and our losses large....Capt. Joseph Mason of Co. G, was killed on Sunday, by a piece of shell....He was one of the best officers in the Regiment and his loss is deeply felt."[100] The *Republican* also marked his death: "He was a genial, warm hearted man, and a brave and efficient officer....His enlistment in a Lansing Company made him regarded as one of our own soldiers, and he has here a large circle of friends that mourn his loss."[101] Nelson Shattuck was also wounded, losing a finger. In early July, the Third Regiment was marching over the dusty roads in intense heat to the Pennsylvania crossroads town of Gettysburg. There they were again hotly engaged, losing forty-one killed, wounded and missing in action. Among the wounded was Sergeant Joseph Stevens.

In the fall of 1863, James Ballard, who had enlisted at age thirty the previous fall, received leave and came home to marry Sarah Pierce of Lansing.[102] Ballard's parents, Appleton and Epiphene, had moved their large family, which grew to ten children, to Lansing in 1848, where Appleton operated a store in Middle Town and a family farm in North Town. Four sons would see action in the war. David, who had moved to Kansas, formed and led Company H, Second Kansas Cavalry, and the other three boys saw action with Lansing-based companies. James enlisted with Company G of the Third; Henry fought with the Second U.S. Sharpshooters, Company B; and Alonzo fought with Company C of the First U.S. Sharpshooters.

While her older brothers were away, L. Anna Ballard, who was born the year the family moved to Lansing, was attending the Female College in Lower Town. Upon graduation, she taught for two years, and while a student of medicine, worked for three years as a drug clerk in the store of Dr. Topping in Dewitt, Michigan. She then studied medicine at the University of Michigan, the Chicago Hospital for Women and Children and the Woman's Medical College of Chicago, receiving her Doctor of Medicine degree in 1878. In 1879, she returned to Lansing and became the city's first female physician, paving the way for the thousands of female doctors who would minister to the medical needs of Lansing for the next 150 years. Among many prestigious positions, Dr. Ballard served as secretary and later as president of the Lansing Medical Society and was instrumental in getting legislation passed to increase the age of consent in Michigan and to protect abused women and children.[103]

Their original three-year enlistment having expired, in the early months of 1864, the remaining Lansing men of Company G began returning home, some to stay and twenty-two of them, those who had agreed to reenlist, for a thirty-day furlough. In addition to the thirty days leave, those reenlisting were promised a one-hundred-dollar signing bonus from the city of Lansing, in part to avoid the necessity of drafting men to fill the local quota under the conscription act. Through a bureaucratic bungle, these men were not given the bonus, nor were they given an extra fifty-dollar bonus recently approved by the Michigan legislature. "Through the dishonesty of some interested person…the whole company are deceived, for it looks to them…as if we are going to find ourselves minus a local bounty.…We were *sold*."[104]

By May 1864, the regiment was engaged in the numerous battles of General Grant's Overland Campaign. The casualty lists printed in the *Republican* were frequent and long, with twenty-two casualties in Company G from May to July: Lieutenant Jerome Ten Eyck, wounded; Sergeant Allen Shattuck, arm shattered; Daniel Shattuck, wounded; John Elliott, killed in action at the Battle of Spotsylvania Court House. The Elliott family lived in the Third Ward, where John's father was a blacksmith. The Ballard family also received tragic news: James had died in the field from a heart attack as the regiment was going into the Battle of the Wilderness. Corporal George Randall also died at the Wilderness on May 5, 1864. Randall was twenty-seven and, before the war, a First Ward machinist living with his wife, Mary, who was a dressmaker. Edgar Clark was wounded in the left leg, leading to an amputation and his discharge from the service. Even with his recent amputation, there was no dissuading Clark: he fully supported President Lincoln in the fall election and "a vigorous prosecution of the war."[105] When Clark died in Lansing in 1902, his death certificate gave the cause of death as the spread of infection from an abscess on the stump of his amputation.[106] Daniel Shattuck was captured during the Battles of Petersburg in June and died one year later in a Confederate prison at Columbia, South Carolina. Lieutenant Charles Price of Lansing was also captured but survived the hellhole of the POW camps and returned to the regiment at the end of the war.

The remnants of the Third (the equivalent of four companies, composed of the men who had reenlisted) were consolidated with the Fifth Michigan Infantry Regiment by special order of the War Department on June 13, 1864,[107] and Company G was redesignated as Company F, Fifth Michigan

Infantry. The few remaining members of the Lansing companies of the First and Second U.S. Sharpshooters were also consolidated with the Fifth Regiment. In June, John Broad returned, and Allen Shattuck was sent home. Shattuck ostensibly came home to recuperate, but there was no mending the resected left arm, and he never returned to the regiment. He would spend the rest of his life in Lansing, where he was a very active member of the Charles T. Foster Post of the GAR and worked as a postman and house painter. When the 1879 capitol was constructed, his company held the contract to paint the dome, and Shattuck famously painted the daunting heights, along with his crew, with the use of his one good arm.[108]

By the spring of 1864, Homer Thayer had been appointed by President Lincoln as assistant quartermaster and promoted to the rank of captain. The following spring, Thayer was sent to Fort Leavenworth, Kansas, in his capacity as quartermaster for the army. In October 1864, while the Fifth was engaged in the trenches outside of Petersburg, recently promoted captain Jerome Ten Eyck resigned his commission and was honorably discharged, availing himself of the recent regulation allowing officers who had served at least three years to separate from the service. After three years of active service, the Lansing company had the unenviable distinction of having had—save but one—all of its members either dead from disease, killed in combat, missing and presumed prisoners of war or wounded. "All of the other veterans of the company have been wounded from one to five times."[109]

After the fall of Petersburg, the capture of Richmond and the surrender of General Lee's Army of Northern Virginia, in April 1865, the Lansing men slowly made their way home. On July 18, 1865, after they received their final pay in Detroit, the train bearing the boys came into the newly constructed Lansing depot, and they were met by "an escort of citizens, with music by the Band and marched to the American House where a bountiful supper was provided for them….After supper, the soldiers and officers were welcomed in a most cordial manner and…after singing *Old Hundred*, the company dispersed," returning to the homes and families they had left four years earlier, albeit each of them forever changed from their experience of war.[110]

Chapter 4

WE HAVE A RAILROAD

The Railroad and Telegraph Come to Lansing

In the spring of 1861, when Company G of the Third Michigan was forming, the capital city was still without a direct link to the rest of the world. It was without a railroad or telegraph connection to Detroit or any other major Michigan city; the closest rail connection was in the small hamlet of Owosso, thirty miles northeast of Lansing. Without the railroad or telegraph, there was no timely news from the rest of the country and the war, the news and mail coming only by the often-irregular daily stage. "Few places of the size are worse off than Lansing for the news."[111] This inconvenience and humiliation would soon change.

In the 1850s, federal and state acts established land grant railroads. The idea was simple: governments would grant large sections of land to the railroads in return for construction of the lines. The railroads could then use the land as collateral for loans or the sale of bonds. Once the roads were completed, the company could sell the land to cover its financial responsibilities.[112] In 1857, the Amboy, Lansing and Traverse Bay Railroad Company was incorporated as a land grant railroad, with the ambitious goal of constructing a line from Amboy in Hillsdale County to Traverse Bay on Lake Michigan. As first proposed, the line ran directly through Lansing, but under pressure from local promoters and to great consternation and criticism, the line instead was built to Owosso. Due to its crooked route, the line was dubbed the "Ram's Horn Railroad."[113] Others insisted the railroad's acronym, ALTB, actually stood for "Awfully Long and Terribly Bumpy."[114] Pressure was applied almost immediately for a connecting "spur" to the capital.

In 1859, the company had 160 hands at work, and William Innes was hired as the superintendent of construction while residing in Lansing.[115] Innes, a veteran of the Mexican-American War, "was a respected railroad surveyor and civil engineer from Grand Rapids whose labors had taken him throughout the state."[116] He learned his engineering skills as a laborer on the Erie Railroad and as a civil engineer for the Oakland and Ottawa Railroad, and he was responsible for a line running from Ada, Michigan, to Lake Michigan. He contracted with the Amboy, Lansing and Traverse Bay Railroad to build the line from Owosso to Lansing. In surveying the road, he discovered a massive sinkhole blocking the route, and he convinced the owners of the company to invest considerable capital to span it. The

Amboy, Lansing and Traverse Bay Railroad construction engineer William P. Innes. *Grand Rapids Public Library*.

project was suspended in 1860, and instead, Innes built a wagon road to carry passengers the remaining few miles from the track to Lansing. The company was furious with Innes for the wasted expense, and he was fired.[117] "In retaliation, he threatened to take all the company's survey records with him. His efforts were frustrated when company officials secured the records and locked them up."[118]

One year later, in September 1861, Innes was commissioned colonel of the First Michigan Engineers and Mechanics Regiment, ending the war as a respected brevet brigadier general.[119] The Engineers recruited in Lansing with an office over the Bagley Grocery Store.[120] At least six recruits were from the city, including Sergeant Silas Hastings. Hastings was a carpenter living in the First Ward with his wife and five-year-old son.[121] He died in July 1863 and was buried in Mississippi, with a later funeral rite at the Lansing Baptist Church. The *State Republican* announced "the death of another of those who have gone forth from our midst in defense of their country."[122] In 1912, a monument to the regiment was erected on the grounds of the 1879 capitol, paid in part by the city of Lansing in tribute to its veterans.

Meanwhile, work on the massive sinkhole continued. By 1861, the track was laid across the marsh and the road, only two and a half miles from

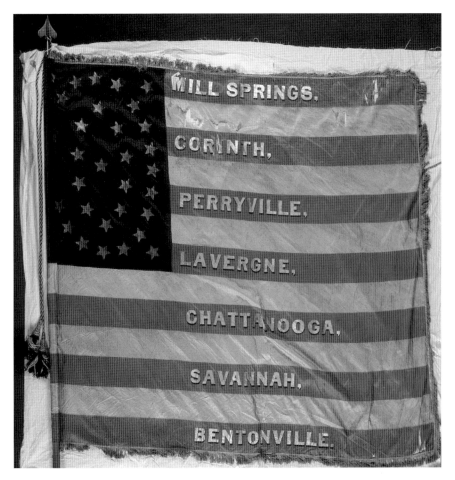

Battle flag of the First Michigan Engineers and Mechanics Regiment. *Save the Flags.*

Lower Town, with sufficient iron on hand to finish the job. The company then pleaded for a $3,000 loan from the citizens of Lansing to complete the project, with bonds filed in the Lansing banking office of J.C. Bailey and Company. A committee of prominent Lansing businessmen including John Kerr, J.C. Bailey and Mayor William Chapman encouraged citizens to buy the bonds. "We earnestly urge the citizens of Lansing and vicinity, to make a vigorous effort for the completion of this road....It is a question of vital importance to the whole community....We shall have a telegraph, a home market for wheat, wool…and hale the day when the Capital came out of the woods."[123] Not to mention the importance of the road for the legislature meeting at the seat of state government.

The monument to the First Michigan Engineers and Mechanics Regiment was placed on the northeast grounds of the state capitol in Lansing in 1912. *Michigan State Capitol Collection, David Marvin.*

By 1862, the road had slowly inched its way to within a mile and a half of Lower Town and thereby secured the arrival of the daily eastern mails by five o'clock. In April, the *Republican* "stated again for the twentieth time…all that is now necessary to be done…is for the citizens of Lansing to furnish the grading—can it be done?"[124] By May, the gangs were again at work on the sinkhole, attempting to fill it, in anticipation of Lansing being in "communication with the rest of mankind."[125] In August, subscriptions raised for the completion of the road were transferred to a committee of citizens, relinquishing to them the burden of completing the project, with the committee again exhorting the citizens, "Shall we not see a railroad to Lansing this Fall?"[126]

By late August, the sinkhole was filled and a foundation set for the 640-foot spanning bridge, in hopes that by the fall harvest, the local farmers would be able to finally bring their crops to Lansing for shipment. By October, however, the road was still unfinished, with concern not about the bridge but rather the foundation. "It looks to us as though more logs, brush and dirt were necessary in the central sink, to give the bridge a broader foundation."[127] But the cars were run without incident, and finally, Lansing could simply declare in a one-line newspaper announcement on November 5, 1862, "The iron is laid into the city, and we now have a Railroad. Hurrah!"[128] Work on the construction of another railroad commenced almost immediately, and the road to Mason and Jackson was opened in the spring of 1866.

The telegraph, which under normal circumstances would have arrived soon after the rights of way were established and a railroad was constructed, was equally slow to materialize. By January 1863, the posts had not been set, and no lines had been strung. "Why don't we have a telegraph line.…We need it, and unless we are unlike every other community which has a railroad, we shall soon have it.…Let somebody move in the matter at once."[129] To no avail, later that month, recognizing it was of the utmost importance for the capital city of Michigan to have the telegraph, Wayne County state representative Thomas W. Lockwood[130] introduced a joint resolution to provide $500 to aid the project, with the state being reimbursed by the rates charged for the use of the line.[131] In September, the plan was to raise $1,500 for the Union Telegraph Company through the sale of subscriptions to future customers, and by October, the requisite number of subscriptions had been sold.[132] By December, the poles were set as far as the town of Bath, and "but a short time will probably elapse before Lansing will be connected with the world."[133] At Christmas, there was a strong possibility Santa would send his yuletide greeting over the Lansing telegraph, but it was not until sometime in January

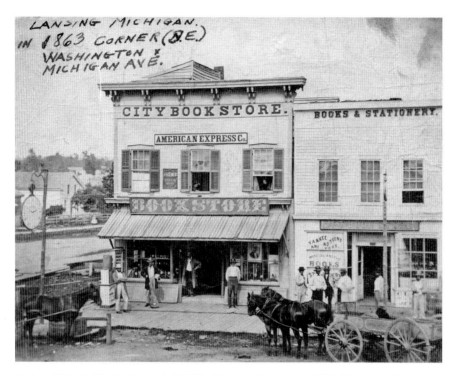

Andrew Vieles's City Bookstore in Middle Town on the corner of Washington and Michigan Avenues, the site of Lansing's first telegraph office. *Forest Parke Library and Archives, Capital Area District Library.*

1864 that the first telegram was sent and received from Andrew Vieles's City Bookstore in Middle Town, on the corner of Washington and Michigan. A telegram to Detroit cost forty cents per ten words, with additional words at three cents each, in addition to a three-cent government tax. "So, it seems some things can be done in Lansing as well as others."[134]

Chapter 5

The Best of Friends Must Part

The Organization of the First and Second U.S. Sharpshooters, Companies C and B

On June 15, 1861, New York engineer, inventor and renowned marksman Hiram Berdan received approval from the U.S. secretary of war, Simon Cameron, to form a special regiment of marksmen. The companies of these highly qualified and tested soldiers were to be hand-selected from across the loyal states of the Union.[135] Printed circulars were soon distributed by the adjutant generals in these states outlining the stringent requirements for enlistment into this special regiment. "No man be accepted who cannot, at 200 yards, put ten consecutive shots in a target, the average distance not to exceed five inches from the center of the bullseye."[136]

The hope was to bring together into one regiment the very best marksmen of the North and to arm them with the best and most reliable rifles. The camp of instruction was at Weehawken, New Jersey, and Companies C, I and K of what came to be known as the First U.S. Sharpshooters Regiment were recruited in Michigan. Later, the Second U.S. Sharpshooters Regiment also formed, and Company B of this regiment organized in Michigan. The "Sharps" shooters were ostensibly named after Christian Sharps, the manufacturer of the Sharps rifle, then in use by Berdan. Of the combined eighteen companies of these two elite regiments, four were recruited in Michigan, two of them partially in Lansing and Ingham County, and several officer's commissions were awarded to men from the capital city.

The regiments of U.S. Sharpshooters were not only unique for their marksmanship, but they were also well known and easily recognized by their unusual uniforms. While most Union infantrymen wore sky blue trousers and dark blue frock coats, the U.S. Sharpshooters wore a dark green coat and cap with a dark plume. Buttons were of dark, hardened rubber and not polished brass. Their trousers were originally of sky blue but were later changed to dark green to match the coat; leather leggings and a knapsack of hair-covered calfskin completed the ensemble. It was thought the green uniforms would better serve as camouflage, but the uniform arguably also contributed to the esprit de corps of these regiments. "When fully uniformed and equipped, the Sharpshooters made a very handsome appearance more so upon the whole, than many others."[137]

On Wednesday, July 24, 1861, an advertisement appeared in the *Lansing State Republican* announcing Colonel William Hammond of the state military board would be in the city to hold an inspection for those "desirous of enlisting in Berdan's famous regiment of Sharpshooters....It is requisite that a string of fifty inches be made in ten shots at a distance of 200 yards."[138] Among the Lansing men to turn out for the test was James Baker. Baker was a twenty-two-year-old chairmaker and painter who moved to Lansing from Richland County, Ohio, with his father, mother and siblings sometime around 1850, when he was ten years old.[139] The Bakers built a home on the corner of Shiawassee Street and Washington Avenue in Middle Town.[140] Baker's father, Harvey, established himself as a chairmaker[141] and later as a partner in the photography business of Alonzo M. Cheney and Harvey Baker.[142] James secured a position as the foreman in the chair-caning department of the State Reform School for Boys.

Apparently, James found time to hone his skills as a rifleman in the howling wilderness surrounding the capital city. He recorded a string of twenty-four inches and was immediately accepted into the corps, mustering in as second lieutenant, Company C, First U.S. Sharpshooters Regiment on August 21, 1861.[143] Marksmanship must have run in the family, for on the same day, James's eighteen-year-old brother Albert registered a string of thirty-four inches and also mustered into the company with the rank of sixth corporal; he would later serve with the Eighth and Eleventh Michigan Cavalry Regiments.[144] Two and a half years later, one of the youngest Baker boys, Oscar, also enlisted, but in the other Lansing U.S. Sharpshooters company, mustering in as an eighteen-year-old private in February 1864 in Company B, Second U.S. Sharpshooters.[145] An August 21, 1861 *Lansing State Republican* account stated, "About a dozen Sharpshooters have left our city during the past week to join Col. Berdan's Regiment. They are made up chiefly of young men—an intelligent, active, first-class set of fellows—who will give a good account of themselves."[146] The absence of their boys must have

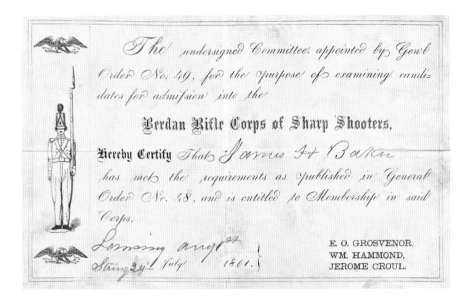

Above: Certificate of marksmanship, James H. Baker. *Clements Library, University of Michigan, Baker Collection.*

Right: Lieutenant James H. Baker, First U.S. Sharpshooters Regiment, Company C. *Clements Library, University of Michigan, Baker Collection.*

been keenly felt at the Lansing home of Harvey and Margaret Baker. This emptiness was only increased by the enlistment of their Lansing nephew by marriage Matthew Elder and his brothers Joseph and John, Joseph joining the Sharpshooters and John and Matthew forming in Lansing the Elder Zouaves Company of the Eighth Michigan Volunteer Infantry Regiment.

The summer of 1861 found Lansing resident John "Jack" Whitman contemplating his future. In July, he had spent time at the Camp of Instruction at Fort Wayne in Detroit,[147] attempting to improve his chances of receiving an officer's commission in one of the newly formed Michigan regiments. Numerous friends and associates had enlisted in Lansing companies that had already left for camps of instruction or the seat of war. At twenty-nine, Jack was living in the Third Ward and was a new husband and father of a three-year-old son. He was very active in the city, serving on the Third Ward Committee on Vigilance, as the first assistant fireman of the Volunteer Rescue Hook and Ladder Company[148] and, later, as the second assistant engineer of the newly formed Lansing Fire Department.[149] He was also an active member of the Masonic Lodge and served as the secretary of the Lansing Independent Order of Odd Fellows.[150]

Whitman was very involved in local and state politics. He supported the formation of the newly created Republican Party and was a delegate to the Republican County Convention in 1860.[151] He served on the executive committee of the Lincoln Wide Awake Club and as a member of the Lansing Young Republicans.[152] This was in addition to the time he spent as a member of the Common Council of Lansing[153] and as the press foreman in the office of the *Lansing State Republican*.[154]

On August 25, 1861, Whitman mustered in as a first lieutenant, Company B, Second U.S. Sharpshooters Regiment. Just one week prior to his mustering in and recognizing the dangerous duty upon which he was about to enter, he arranged to "make, publish and declare" his last will and testament, written in his own hand. He bequeathed to his wife, Marietta, executrix of the estate, all his real and personal estate. The will was witnessed by his Lansing friends—Smith Hunter and Stephen Bingham.[155] Bingham was a Lansing attorney and partner in the firm of Dart and Bingham and received his law degree from the University of Michigan. He later served intermittently as the editor of the *Lansing State Republican* and as Lansing postmaster. In 1888, he wrote the *Early History of Michigan.*

Among the other Lansing officers of the "Wolverine Sharpshooters," as Company B had taken to calling themselves, was twenty-two-year-old second lieutenant Darius Calkins. Calkins moved to Lansing in 1859 from Adrian

Lieutenant John J. "Jack" Whitman, Second U.S. Sharpshooters Regiment, Company B. *Brian T. White Collection.*

and was working as a dry goods clerk prior to his enlistment.[156] Before leaving for the field, he was presented with a Colt's six-shooter pistol with an eight-inch rifled barrel. The presentation was made by the Reverend C.S. Armstrong on behalf of the sabbath school of the Lansing Presbyterian Church. It might seem somewhat unusual and contradictory that a church sabbath school should present an implement of death to a parishioner, but Reverend Armstrong professed, in his presentation speech, that the pistol was "an effective weapon with which to meet the enemies of our country, who are fighting for a barbarism disgraceful to God and man… that it was a present of which the recipient will prove himself worthy."[157] Whether the "barbarism" was a reference to secession or slavery, there was no question where the good Reverend's loyalty lay.

Official presentation ceremonies of regimental and company battle flags and officers' swords and pistols were a common occurrence in many small towns across Michigan, especially in the early days of the war. The regimental companies, both North and South, recruited and formed in small communities: these men knew and were often related to each other, so the flags and arms presented were a link to their hometowns. These communities were extremely proud of "their boys," and so the accoutrements they provided to the men were a constant reminder of their families and friends back home and of the communities from which they came and for which they were fighting—and dying. Lansing was no exception.

In late September 1861, Lieutenant Whitman was the recipient of a handsomely mounted revolver presented to him by his comrades in the office of the *Lansing State Republican*. In presenting the revolver, the publisher, John Kerr, and the editor, I.M. Cravath (who later organized and led into the field Lansing-based Company G of the Twelfth Michigan Volunteer Infantry Regiment), stated they could not

permit you to take your leave without some fitting token of the kindly feelings cherished toward you and of the lively interest taken in your welfare.…Be assured that you shall ever have our heartfelt wishes for your safety, and speedy return. Accept this revolver as a slight token of the estimation of your old co-laborers and associates. We know that it will be your constant companion and trust it will oft remind you of those who now present it to you.[158]

In his reply, Whitman stated:

It is with heartfelt thanks that I accept the generous gift this day bestowed upon me….I cannot but feel that I am parting with old and tried friends; but the best of friends must part and so with us….It may be the means of saving the life of the recipient, and also of corresponding destruction to the enemies of our country….I shall keep it as long as I remain a soldier, if possible, and hope to return to you in due time, with this gift as a companion….I bid you an affectionate farewell.[159]

The captain of Company B was Andrew Stuart, entering into the command at the relatively advanced age of thirty-nine. Stuart was working as an upholsterer and living in Lansing's First Ward when he received his commission.[160] His time in the service, however, was limited, as he resigned his commission less than one year later and just one week after his company and regiment were hotly engaged at the Battle of Antietam, Maryland, on September 17, 1862. One wonders if the carnage of America's single bloodiest day and the loss of numerous men from his company contributed to his decision to resign. According to Whitman, in a letter home the previous June, Stuart had suffered a debilitating bout of typhoid fever and was not well. Stuart returned to Lansing and opened a furniture and chair shop. Although he was honorably discharged, there must have been some question regarding his resignation. The March 16, 1864 edition of the *Lansing State Republican* reported his furniture shop was assaulted by a part of Company B, Second U.S. Sharpshooters, prior to their departure for Detroit. The veterans, who were presumably home on their thirty-day furlough after having reenlisted, "having a grudge against him for wrongs which they alleged they had suffered while under his command, determined to chastise him personally, but failing to find him, they destroyed some of his chairs and broke his windows."[161]

In late August 1861, the companies of the First U.S. Sharpshooters left Detroit, before receiving their uniforms and equipment,[162] and on October 5, 1861, Company B of the Second U.S. Sharpshooters also left Detroit, similarly without having been issued uniforms or equipment. In his year of service, Jack Whitman became a faithful camp correspondent to his young family in Lansing and to his friends in the office of the *Republican.* In a letter home, from their camp of instruction on a high bluff at Weehawken, New Jersey, Whitman said the boys "were obliged to sleep the first night without blankets, which caused a number of us to take slight colds.…A few of the boys have the diarrhea and a trifle of the ague"[163]—a harbinger of the sickness and death from disease awaiting them. Despite sleeping on the cold ground, Whitman reported from their camp overlooking New York City, "The boys are enjoying themselves finely, and all seem well pleased with the soldier's life."[164] The hope was they would receive their uniforms and rifles before commencing to their rendezvous in the nation's capital.

In a letter home in late October, Lieutenant Whitman wrote of the trials and tribulations of traveling on the railroads from Weehawken to Washington, riding on "very poor and uncomfortable class of cars…having been shoved and backed around upon all the side-tracks of two or three different lines of roads…on a freight train variously estimated by many to be from one-half to two and half miles in length, and all the cars nearly filled with soldiers." When finally approaching D.C., "the sight of the tents and the soldiers as we passed them gave us such a feeling of delight that we could not keep from swinging our hats and cheering at the top of our voices."[165] From their camp about two miles north of the Capitol, Lieutenant Whitman bemoaned that the majority of the Sharpshooters had still not received their rifles. "The Colonel was called on the other day for three companies of Sharp-shooters to go over the Potomac, and I understand he told them as soon as their rifles were ready the men could go into service, and not before."[166]

Company B left Michigan sixteen men short, so Lieutenant Calkins returned to Lansing on a recruiting detail and set up his office in the Benton House in Upper Town.[167] He soon enlisted the men needed to fill out the one-hundred-man company and was off to rendezvous with the remainder of Company B at their encampment near Washington, D.C. In a November 20 letter to his friends at the newspaper, Lieutenant Whitman reported the regiment was marching six to eight hours every day, except on Sunday, and expressed his frustration with the lack of weapons and full uniforms. He also gave an update on promotions of the Lansing boys in his company, including William Ostrum and Asa Shattuck.[168] Shattuck had recently transferred from Company C of the First USSS to Company B of the Second USSS.

There were dozens of Michigan companies and regiments in camps of instruction in and around Washington, D.C., and often the men, especially the officers, took the opportunity to visit with friends from their hometowns who were encamped nearby. Whitman reported visiting with the boys of the First Michigan Cavalry Regiment, especially his friends Lieutenant H.E. Hascall and L.D.F. Poore, with whom he formerly worked in the office of the *Lansing State Republican*. Seventy men from Lansing would enlist and fight with numerous Michigan cavalry units, including the First, Third, Fourth, Fifth, Sixth, Seventh, Ninth, Tenth and Eleventh Regiments. Whitman also reported that Lansing men Mr. Siverd and Corporal Shattuck of the Third Michigan Infantry Regiment came over to visit the camp and the Lansing boys of the sharpshooter companies and, one may surmise, held a unique and special family reunion with his father and brother. Whitman stated, "Messrs. Russell and Winter, both of Lansing, dined with us today, and judging from the circle of faces which surrounded us at one time, a resident of Lansing of three months ago, might have easily deceived himself as to his whereabouts."[169] Asa Winter had received an appointment and was serving in D.C. as an acting paymaster,[170] and F.G. Russell was a friend and former teacher in the Second Ward in Lansing[171] who was now working in D.C. in the Department of the Interior.[172] Russell, too, became a regular correspondent to the *Lansing State Republican* and one year later would be asked to complete a final act of friendship for his friend from Lansing. In the same letter, Whitman provided an update on the Lansing men who had enlisted in Company C, First U.S. Sharpshooters, and reported: "Lieut. J.H. Baker, Van Etten, Kelsey, Wiser, and the others from Lansing in the first Michigan Company are well…and are as fat as fools, and say they never felt better in their lives."[173]

Lieutenant Whitman and his men must have longed for the normal routine of their old preenlistment life in Lansing. Soon an event occurred allowing him and his men to exercise their civilian avocation. The normal quiet of an early December Sabbath morning in the camp of the Sharpshooters was interrupted by the cry of "fire." Colonel Berdan's headquarters building had caught fire. According to Whitman, "The Lansing fire department was tolerably well represented on the occasion…and none did more service, leaving me to judge, than ours.…We were the first on the ground and threw the first water."[174] In the same letter home, Whitman espoused the eternal soldier's lament of the lack of pay due to the men. When mustering in, the companies were assured by state officials they would receive pay from the day of enrollment in Michigan. The federal paymaster, however, only paid the men for one month and three days, arguing the men would have to receive the balance owed them from the State of Michigan. This missing pay was no doubt a burden to the men and to their families back home in Lansing. Whitman stated: "It seems hard that soldiers cannot take the word of government officials in those regards, but they must subject themselves either to loss or great inconvenience in getting simply their just dues."[175] Whitman must have felt some satisfaction in reading his own published letter in his hometown paper, as the boys received the *Lansing State Republican* regularly in the mail. This lack of pay issue was published in the leading newspaper of Michigan's capital city and no doubt would fall on the eyes of state officials.

On Christmas Day 1861, the faithful correspondent again gave an update to the citizens of Lansing on the prospects and conditions of the boys in the sharpshooter regiments still encamped in the environs of D.C. To the *Republican*, Whitman reported the boys were still encamped on their old ground and living in tents "just as though it were warm and pleasant."[176] He further reported the consequences of living in such conditions was a slight cold for about one-fifth of the company. Humor being the best remedy in such situations, Whitman stated the colds were "generally cured promptly by our distinguished Surgeon sometime between the time of attack by the disease and the death of the patient, the exact time not yet having transpired, as he has not cured the first case."[177] The lack of arms being a sore point, Whitman again used humor to address the issue: "But one company in our regiment is fully armed at present: the Minnesota, and they are armed with bows and arrows. Our company expect to be armed with slings, and the boys are on tip-toe at the prospect of having something to fight with.… The balance of the regiment will be armed as best suites their taste, either brickbats, stones or clubs."[178] Appropriately, in the gift-giving season, Whitman sent thanks to the Ladies Military Aid Society of Lansing for the supply of towels and "housewives" (sewing kits) delivered from Lansing by Lieutenant Calkins.

By January 1862, the vast majority of the men still had not received their arms but were in anticipation of receiving the new Spencer's magazine rifle, as reported by the *Republican*. The advantage of these new repeating rifles was they could be loaded once with a multiple-round magazine "in almost the same time the ordinary (single shot, muzzle loaded) musket can be loaded," fired multiple times and "neither caps nor primers are required, the detonating powder being in a metal cartridge with the powder and ball."[179] According to the same article, the rifles had been ordered for the regiments on the personal request of the commanding general of the Army of the Potomac, George B. McClellan. This article was in error, because the Spencer's rifles were never issued; it was not until much later in the war that these rifles came into use.[180] Whitman again lamented: "We are yet here unarmed, as we have been for nearly three months. We have nearly given up all hopes of seeing any weapons of war for our own use."[181]

As the regiments eagerly awaited their full equipment and weapons, sickness and death reared its ugly head, as they were wont to do in Civil War encampments. Diseases spread like wildfire among the encamped men. Most had never been exposed to, nor had the opportunity to build natural immunity to, many diseases prior to their enlistment. Whitman reported "with deep regret that…about the middle of December the measles made its appearance in our camp, and in the course of ten days we had a few cases, which spread among our boys.…Our future was doomed to bring death in the most heartrending manner possible."[182] In a report filed in January 1862, Charles S. Tripler, a Detroiter and the medical director for the Army of the Potomac, stated that "measles which seem to be scourging the whole army of the United States, still break out from time to time.…Berdan's Sharpshooters have been and are still severely affected by that disease."[183] The first noncombat deaths were reported. Succumbing to disease: Silas Lindsley from Dansville, George Lewis of Oneida, Corporal John Hunt of Onondaga, Nelson Leslie of Meridian and William Ostrum and Sylvanus Piersons of the city of Lansing, all of Company B, Second U.S. Sharpshooters "Thus in less than eight days we have lost six of our company…and the country has lost the services of six as good soldiers as ever enlisted to fight her battles."[184] The boys were laid to rest in the burying ground of the "Old Soldiers Home," and Whitman said, "A more solemn and melancholy scene, I must say, I have never yet witnessed and I trust I never shall be called upon to witness its like again."[185] Sadly, this was but the first of many solemn and melancholy scenes to come.

As their ranks were diminished by sickness and death, "a ministering angel appeared, in the person of Miss A.C. Rogers, who has been very busy in endeavoring to find comfortable quarters for our sick in the city for the last four days."[186] The appearance of Miss Rogers—who, along with her sister, Delia Rogers, founded the Michigan Female College in Lower Town in Lansing—brought some much-needed comfort to the men. "She has worked like a hero.…She is certainly deserving of all praise for her efforts, as she has worked with a will, fully worthy of the woman. She may rest assured that her visits will be remembered while life lasts, by all who comprise company B."[187] Despite the losses, still the Lansing men of Company B remained unarmed and ill-equipped. "There must be a shameful dereliction of duty in the War

Department, when these regiments, of which the larger portion have been in the field more than three months, are not yet furnished with arms…The very best men in the service and those most needed in case of an advance are thus of no use in emergency but are left to die in camp, without seeing service, or in any way aiding the government in whose behalf they have sought a position of danger."[188]

During the winter of 1862, several of the officers of Companies B and C returned to Lansing on leave and to recruit soldiers. Lieutenant Baker returned and, while on leave in the city, married the former Ednah Desano on February 23, 1862.[189] In early March, Lieutenant Calkins came home "on a short visit to his friends in the city. He is not enjoying first rate health—but hopes after a few days quiet to be able to join the company."[190] By the following month, however, after a twenty-day furlough,[191] he was forced to "resign his commission on account of sickness and returned to the city."[192] "The absence of Capt. Stewart, and the sickness of Lieut. Calkins, has left the command of the Wolverine Sharpshooters upon Lieut. Whitman.…All the men are anxious for active service."[193]

In early March, Lieutenant Whitman retuned home for a short furlough and to recruit extra men for his company. "Jack is in first rate health and

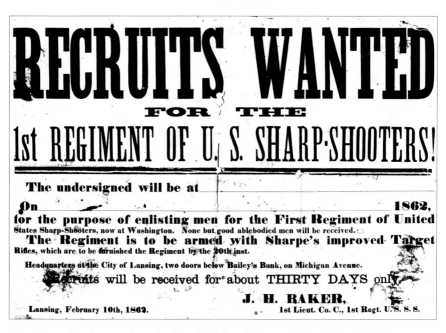

Recruiting advertisement from the *State Republican*, February 1862. *Archives of Michigan.*

is anxious to get thirty good reliable wolverines for the Lansing Company. Boys now is your chance."[194] In their camps just outside of Washington, the Sharpshooters had finally received their Colt's rifled muskets and were expecting an order to advance soon. On March 20, the long-awaited order arrived, and the First Sharpshooter regiment proceeded with the Army of the Potomac to the Siege of Yorktown, Virginia, and the numerous battles of the Peninsula Campaign.[195] The Second Sharpshooters soon followed into the field and proceeded to Falmouth, Virginia. The regiments and the men of Lansing were about to experience their first real test under fire. Boys, now is your chance!

Chapter 6

THE LADIES OF LANSING

The Ladies Military Aid Society and the Young Ladies Loyal League of Lansing

The visit of Abigail Rogers of the Michigan Female College of Lansing to the field encampment of the Second U.S. Sharpshooters was an example of the unwavering support Lansing citizens provided to the troops. This support included large bounties to assist the families of men who enlisted, free medical care for soldiers' families offered by physicians H.T. Hawley in Middle Town and C.A. Jeffries in Lower Town,[196] increased taxes to support soldiers' families, local farmers who supplied horses to the cavalry, days of fasting and prayer and the even more tangible support offered specifically by the ladies of Lansing. Early in the war, ladies' military aid societies formed throughout the country, and Lansing was no exception. The federal government eventually relied heavily upon the money and materials donated by these citizen-run volunteer organizations. "Mothers, wives and sweethearts collected and sent articles of comfort and supplies of necessity to their boys in blue."[197]

Recognizing the efforts of these nascent societies and the need for a central system of organization, in June 1861, President Lincoln authorized the formation of the United States Sanitary Commission (USSC). Under the leadership of General Secretary Frederick Law Olmsted, the commission, which eventually grew to twenty-one members, was charged "to inquire into the subjects of diet, clothing, cooks, camping grounds, in fact everything connected with the prevention of disease among volunteer soldiers not accustomed to the rigid regulations of the regular troops…and to discover methods by which private and unofficial interest and money might supplement the appropriations of the Government."[198]

It has been estimated that these civilian, private, charitable organizations, many working through the auspices of the USSC, provided up to 90 percent of the medicines dispensed to sick and wounded soldiers, as well as ton after ton of bandages, lint to pack wounds, tents, cots, blankets, pillows, towels, housewives (sewing kits), havelocks (head and neck shrouds), quilts, shirts and socks. Donations were not limited to medicines and clothing but also included dried and fresh vegetables, meats, catsup, applesauce, cider, honey, canned and dried fruits (especially blackberries and cranberries), jellies, tobacco, horseradish and medicinal wine and brandy. Over twenty thousand aid organizations were formed in the North, and the women raised almost $5 million in funds and $15 million worth of goods.[199]

The ladies' aid societies also offered support to the soldiers' needy families. The average monthly pay of a Union private was $13. In good times, when that pay, or at least a portion of it, made its way home, it was infrequently enough for the families to subsist on, making the assistance offered by these benevolent organizations essential. In November 1861, the Ingham County Board of Supervisors reported that of the ninety-five families whose fathers or sons had enlisted, sixty-six of them had requested aid.[200] The $7,416 county fund had been raised by special levy.

One of the first advertisements for a meeting of the Lansing Ladies Military Aid Society appeared in June 1861, shortly after the war started. The ladies met in Dodge's Hall on Washington Avenue to organize and prepare a strawberry festival to be held in the capitol chamber of the house of representatives. The chambers and offices of the old capitol were frequently used for church services, entertainment and large meetings, a practice that would continue after the new capitol was completed in 1879. The proceeds of the strawberry festival went toward the purchase of material to sew havelocks for the men. The festival raised almost sixty dollars, allowing the ladies to purchase enough material to sew havelocks for 150 men.[201] This festival was but the first of dozens of festivals, sanitary fairs, special dinners, where oysters and ice cream were available but at an extra charge, benefit concerts and lectures and special "Soldiers Suppers" for the boys home on leave, sponsored by the society and later by the Young Ladies Loyal League.

While the editor of the *State Republican*, I.M. Cravath, was appreciative of the ladies' efforts, in October he editorialized: "Many women have the notion that they have nothing to do in saving the country. This is a great mistake....Their services are invaluable in procuring supplies of clothing, etc. without which the privations of camp life are more to be dreaded than the iron hail of battle....It is a matter of imperative necessity that every loyal woman should do what lies in her power to furnish such things as are absolutely required."[202] Later that same month, Cravath would organize and lead into the field Lansing Company G of the Twelfth Michigan Volunteer Infantry Regiment, taking to heart his own admonition to the ladies of Lansing that they contribute to the war effort.

Soon after the war began, Harriet (Edgerton) Tenney was elected president of the society and continued to hold that position until the close of the war. "She devoted the most of her time in the rooms of the society in the old capitol, looking after the welfare, and providing aid for the soldiers on the tented fields and in the hospitals."[203] Tenney was born in Essex, Vermont, in 1834. She received her education at the Franklin Academy and, after marrying Jesse Eugene Tenney, moved to Calhoun County, Michigan, where they both were engaged in teaching. They then moved to Marshall and took charge of the Union School there, later moving to Lansing when Jesse was appointed as the state librarian, a role Harriet would later occupy for twenty-two years, becoming the first female state officer in Michigan.

Throughout the war, the *Republican* frequently contained a weekly report of the activities of the Lansing Ladies Military Aid Society. This report was filed by the treasurer, Sarah Dart. Her husband was prominent Lansing attorney, Rollin Dart, of the firm Dart and Bingham. These detailed reports included a full accounting of every cent raised and spent and every donated article. The secretary was Laura Pratt, who was married to Hubert R. Pratt, a clerk in the auditor general's office. The Pratts were living in the Second Ward, and Laura was very active in the ladies' aid society. Her husband would later become deputy state auditor general, a role he filled for over twenty years.[204] In the later years of the war, Laura Pratt became the "packing secretary," and a Mrs. E.R. Hunter became secretary.

Many of the members had brothers, fathers or husbands who were serving in the field, and they came from the working and professional classes. Among the members was Emily (Seymour) Armstrong, whose husband, the Reverend Chester Armstrong, was pastor of Lansing's First Presbyterian Church.[205] In the last year of the war, he served as the chaplain

Harriet Tenney, president of the Ladies Military Aid Society of Lansing. *Jacob McCormick Collection.*

of the Fourth Michigan Volunteer Cavalry Regiment.[206] A detachment of this regiment captured the fleeing president of the Confederacy, Jefferson Davis. A Mrs. D.L Case, whose family owned a shop in Lower Town and whose son D.L. Case was serving as a lieutenant in the 102nd New York Infantry, was also a member. Late in the war, her husband, Daniel, was commissioned as a major in the U.S. Army.[207]

Emily (Hewitt) Hull, another contributing and active member, was married to Middle Town physician Dr. Joseph Hull. Dr. Hull served as the examining surgeon on the Ingham County draft board and was commissioned as the assistant surgeon in the First Battalion, First Ohio Sharpshooters Regiment. Upon his return, he served on the Lansing Examining Board for Pensions, assisting many of the wounded veterans, or their survivors, in receiving their much-needed pensions from the federal government.[208]

By October 1862, yielding to the war's demands of procuring sufficient donations, the ladies' aid society resorted to publishing reports in the *Republican*, including the names of the Lansing ladies and citizens who donated funds, food or material. This weekly report included every donated pint of horseradish and pickles and every pair of underwear and socks. Perhaps as important as the names listed were the names that were not, the society not being above a little public adulation or embarrassment to further its cause. Included in the lists were strict instructions on how the food should be prepared and packaged. "All fruits and pickles should be put in tin cans, properly soldered....1 bottle of tomatoes from Mrs. C.W. Coryell and 1 can of peaches from Mrs. C.S. Armstrong, not being properly sealed, have spoiled."[209] Horror of horrors, to have your canning ability judged in such a public forum.

Through the course of the war, collection points varied within the city. Donated articles were to be left at the state house, at A.J. Viele's bookstore, at the room of dressmaker Miranda Edgerly, at T.D. Billings's store and other designated sites, predominantly in Middle Town. Although most shipping was conducted by express, often free or at reduced rates, or through the channels of the United States Sanitary Commission, it appears that early in the war, at least some of the supply transport was through private arrangements. Transport companies working in Michigan advertised regular trips to D.C. and to the front lines and included the firm of John O'Hara and Sons, which guaranteed personal delivery of boxed goods to individual soldiers fighting with the First, Second, Fourth, Eighth, Sixteenth and Twentieth Michigan Regiments. "The goods to be marked to the person, company and regiment with an indelible mark."[210]

Requests for aid and letters of thanks from soldiers were common in the columns of the Lansing paper. As the winter months approached, the soldiers pleaded for warm undergarments, wool socks, mittens and gloves: "As the cold bleak winds of December are now felt in our ranks, I would say to Mrs. R.C. Dart, Treasurer of the Soldier's Aid Society, that a few pairs of gloves would be received with great pleasure."[211] This entreaty was from an orderly of Captain Matthew Elder's Lansing Zouave Company of the Eighth Michigan Volunteer Infantry Regiment. "Our heartfelt thanks to many friends at home, for the kindness of love and friendship contained in three boxes lately received by us.…As each package was brought forth…the light of joy would illume the countenance of the happy recipient perchance followed by the sympathetic tear."[212]

Asa Winter, who was serving in the blockading squadron on the St. James River on the U.S. steamer *E.B. Hale*, near Jacksonville, Florida, regularly received the *Republican* through the mail. In September 1862, he wrote: "Yesterday I received three of your papers.…I do hope that the good people of Lansing will remember the gallant fellows. You don't know how much good, it does me to receive a home paper, or how gladly a box of gentle reminders of home is received. If ever a man thanks God for home and friends it is when he is away from them."[213] Winter had served in multiple roles in Lansing city government and the state auditor's office, as an assistant editor at the *Republican* and also as an engineer and secretary of the Torrent Engine Company No. 1. before accepting a commission as a naval paymaster in August 1861. His views about slavery no doubt led to his enlistment: "So help me God never will I cease preaching the Abolition of slavery."[214] In 1863, he served aboard the blockading flagship *San Jacinto*, near Key West, Florida. In a letter dated June 10, 1864, Winter wrote: "When one thinks of the brave boys who have gone from our midst, fought, died—for what? That we might live."[215] On June 28, Asa Winter died of disease and was buried in the salty sea far from home and the freshwater Great Lakes of Michigan.

Meanwhile, the work of the ladies' aid society continued. Secretary Dart, pleading for an increase in donations, wrote, "Think of those soldiers who have left homes and friends to endure hardships unknown to us sitting here quietly by our firesides."[216] In early January 1863, one A.E.C.—who, although never identified in his letters, was presumably Albert E. Cowles—wrote a lengthy thank-you letter for a six-hundred-pound crate forwarded from home to Lansing-based Company A of the Twentieth Michigan Volunteer Infantry Regiment, with which he was serving. He wrote, "That box of which we had heard so much and for which we had anxiously looked so long, arrived in camp.…If the ladies of Lansing could have witnessed its reception, if, as each received his package or packages, they could have heard and seen the expressions, for as much could be seen as heard, I think they would have been paid for all the trouble it cost them. It would have reminded them of a large family of children anxiously waiting Christmas morning.…We were pleased to find that those who were recruited out of the city were not forgotten."[217]

A children's aid society, a second Lansing ladies' aid society and the Young Ladies Loyal League also operated within the city during the war. The Young Ladies Loyal League was led by its twenty-year-old president and later secretary Fannie Foster, the only daughter of Theodore and Frances Foster. The Young Ladies Loyal League received some unwanted and unwarranted attention in 1863 when the Democratic *Lansing State Journal*, which had recently resumed publishing, accused the league of being an organization committed to assisting Lansing men in evading the draft, claiming that it was raising money for a fund "to pay the exemption fee of any member that may be drafted, and men are solicited to join the League in order thus to escape the Draft."[218] In reply to this accusation, a "Private of the Ladies Loyal League," presumed to be Fannie Foster, wrote: "If you wish to know anything about the proceedings of our League, you may meet us at the Supreme Court room any Wednesday afternoon at 4 o'clock."[219] This open invitation apparently ended the accusations. In 1864, Fannie would marry Albert Cowles, after his disability discharge from service with the Twentieth Michigan Infantry.[220]

Fannie Foster Cowles, president, Young Ladies Loyal League of Lansing. *Collection of Lille Foster.*

In the fall of 1863, the Chicago Northwestern Soldiers' Sanitary Fair was held, proceeds of the fair being contributed to the U.S. Sanitary Commission. Citizens and Lansing-area farmers were encouraged to donate generously to the fair. A reported 134 barrels of vegetables and preserves, totaling 26,400 pounds, were donated, including eleven barrels of vegetables from the State Agricultural College in East Lansing and two large barrels of "excellent sour krout" from the "German ladies," with the Amboy, Lansing and Traverse Bay Railroad providing free shipment.[221]

By the last year of the war, the Lansing soldiers' aid societies had broadened their scope and were donating new and used articles of clothing to refugees and freedmens' associations.[222] Perhaps this was a harbinger of the yet unaccomplished work that lay ahead for the ladies of Lansing and the societies they helped form that contributed so greatly to the Union victory. Many women who volunteered in the ladies' military aid societies went on to participate in and to lead temperance and women's suffrage associations, one example being Fannie Foster, who became president of the Woman's Suffrage Association and served as a delegate to the National Woman's Suffrage convention.[223] By their participation, these women "gained access to the information they craved, and they honed their organizational and political skills,"[224] and "many of these women went on to join suffrage societies after the war, using their legacy of sacrifice and leadership during the war to insist that they should be allowed to vote."[225] Sadly, it would take another fifty-five years of hard work and pitched battles by women before they finally would be allowed to vote nationally with the ratification of the Nineteenth Amendment.

Chapter 7

THEY FOUGHT AS DEMONS

Engaged in Battle, the First and Second U.S. Sharpshooters, Company C and B

While on his recruiting mission in Lansing, Lieutenant Jack Whitman of Company B, Second U.S. Sharpshooters, was sent notice to immediately return to his company in the field. His regiment had received its orders to proceed to Bristoe Station, Virginia, and presumed action. In a letter published in the *Lansing State Republican* on April 23, 1862, Whitman regaled his readers with a description of his long, arduous odyssey from "the quiet city" back to the front with his new recruits in tow. With the absence of a railroad in Lansing (the connection would not be completed until November), Whitman and his men took the stagecoach, which traveled the old plank road daily from Lansing to Detroit. "We left our homes and friends in the city of Lansing and vicinity for the seat of war.… After a long and tedious ride of 10 hours we reached the city of Detroit."[226] Upon his arrival, ninety men were placed under Whitman's command, with orders to proceed to Washington with "a detachment of recruits for the 1st, 2nd, 3rd, 4th and 5th regiments of Michigan Infantry, 1st and 2nd U.S.S.S. and Brodhead's 1st Michigan Cavalry."[227]

From Detroit, the motley band spent three hours on the train to Toledo, another four hours to Cleveland, seven hours to Pittsburgh, ten hours to Harrisburg, six hours to Baltimore and a final four hours to Washington. The trip, now accomplished in approximately nine hours by automobile, took eight days, including layovers and forty-four hours on the stage and train.[228] Lieutenant Whitman's assignment was not yet complete: he had to escort each detachment of recruits to their regiments, encamped throughout Virginia.

On April 12, eighteen days after leaving Lansing, Whitman rejoined his regiment at Falmouth, Virginia, opposite Fredericksburg on the Rappahannock River. There the regiment remained until May 25, when it participated in General Irvin McDowell's advance on the Confederate capital in Richmond and operations against Confederate general Thomas "Stonewall" Jackson. On June 5, 1862, Whitman wrote from Hay Market, Virginia, of a hope destined to be unfulfilled: "If it should so happen that our company ever become engaged in battle, I hope to be allowed to relate some of the circumstances to your readers."[229] From August 16 to September 2, the company supported Union general John Pope's campaign in Northern Virginia, culminating in the Union defeat at the Second Battle of Bull Run on August 30, 1862. In September, Whitman and his men began a march through Maryland that would terminate on the banks of the Antietam Creek and the twenty-four-acre cornfield of D.R. Miller.

While the Second USSS was operating in northern Virginia, the Lansing men of Company C, First USSS, were engaged in the Peninsula Campaign. Lieutenant Baker reported in his daily notebook that the men of his company "were almost constantly doing outpost, picket and skirmish duty."[230] Baker and his men fought continuously, at Yorktown, Williamsburg, Hanover Court House, Mechanicsville, Gaines Mill, Charles City and White Oak Swamp.[231] In a letter to his new bride, Lieutenant Baker reported that at Mechanicsville, "I was in command of the company…where we could not hear ourselves talk for the roar of the cannonading and musketry. We rushed on, and soon found ourselves within 50 feet of the rebels.…We laid in the woods all night amid the wounded and dying, whose groans were almost enough to strike terror to the heart."[232]

As Confederate forces advanced, the Sharpshooters covered the Union army's retreat, destroying the bridges as they fell back to Gaines Mill, where on June 27, according to Baker's account, "was fought one of the hardest battles ever fought by so few men.…The rebels fought fiercely and like demons. They rushed madly upon our men and were cut down like sheep. But they were too many for us, and we were obliged to retreat across the Chickahominy [River], leaving the wounded, or the most of them, on the field."[233] This must have been a most gut-wrenching decision for Lieutenant Baker: to leave his wounded on the field, including boyhood friends from Lansing. Baker concluded his letter with, "Trusting in Him who doeth all things well, I must close and go in search of some more of my men."[234] By August 30, Company C was engaged at the Second Battle of Bull Run, where Corporal Peter Van Etter of Lansing was killed and Baker was slightly wounded. September found them also on the roads of Maryland, destined for a reunion with boyhood friends from Lansing amid the quiet pastures, cornfields and woods of Sharpsburg, Maryland, on September 17, 1862.

Fueled by his recent victory at the Second Battle of Bull Run, the Confederate commander of the Army of Northern Virginia, Robert E. Lee, launched an invasion into Maryland. His purpose was to enlist support for the Southern cause among presumed sympathetic Marylanders, with the hope one more Confederate victory would encourage European support for the fledgling Confederacy. The Union and Confederate armies collided on Wednesday, September 17, 1862, near the town of Sharpsburg on the Antietam Creek, the single bloodiest day in American history. "From sunup to sundown, the battle of Antietam cost approximately 23,110 lives either killed, wounded, missing in action or taken as prisoners of war—nearly two Americans every second."[235] A pivotal part of the battle took place in the twenty-four-acre cornfield of farmer David Miller, north of the Dunker Church on the Hagerstown Pike. The cornfield changed hands no fewer than six times: in the epicenter of the fighting stood Company B of the Second U.S. Sharpshooters under the command of Lieutenant Jack Whitman. The Second USSS was in it hot and heavy, in the thickest of the fight in the cornfield at about sunrise, sustaining a loss at this battle of fully 25 percent of those present for duty.[236] Among the wounded was Lieutenant Jack Whitman, who fell while leading his men.

In the early part of the battle, Whitman was struck by a piece of shell, which tore off the kneecap of his left leg, with no apparent injury to the main bones. He was taken to a home converted to a field hospital in Keedysville, Maryland, near the battlefield. His left leg was then "needlessly" amputated about halfway between the knee and the hip. It was later determined the "reckless, butchering, villainous" surgeon had failed to take up the main artery. The lieutenant became very weak from the loss of blood and lingered until 1:20 on the morning of September 18, when "his noble spirit took its flight to the better world."[237]

Upon the request of Lieutenant Whitman's young widow, Marietta, and the *Republican* publisher John Kerr, F.G. Russell was asked to travel from his new home near Washington, D.C., to the battlefield at Antietam to retrieve the body of his young Lansing friend. Russell traveled to "the ball riddled and shell shattered town" of Sharpsburg the first weekend in October and enlisted the services of an undertaker, a wagon and a team of horses, securing an appropriate metal coffin along the way. Upon his arrival on the

William Denny was twenty-two when he left his job as a gunsmith in Lansing to enlist with the Second U.S. Sharpshooters Regiment. He served to the end of the war, mustering out in July 1865. *Brian T. White Collection.*

"bloody fields," where he observed hundreds of newly dug, shallow graves, he located the camp of the Lansing boys of Company G of the Sixteenth Michigan Infantry and Lieutenant Jacob Webber. The lieutenant saddled some horses and personally escorted Russell to the camp of the Second USSS. The Company B soldiers, including William Denny and Ulysses Ward, along with two other men, took Russell to the cemetery, two miles north of Sharpsburg, where "the gallant Whitman" had been well buried in a good poplar coffin. Denny, who had lived and worked in Lansing as a gunsmith, and Ward, who was a butcher in Lansing's Second Ward,[238] assisted Russell in transferring the badly decomposed remains of their mutual friend and company commander into the metal coffin.

According to Russell in his letter to Kerr, eulogizing Whitman: "Jack's company almost idolized him. His genial, amiable disposition, his familiarity and frank, cheerful deportment towards them, gained the affections of his men, and secured the respect of his fellow officers.…It afforded me pleasure to do Mrs. Whitman so great a favor, but it saddened me to be under the painful necessity of forwarding to you the mutilated remains of so excellent a friend, so brave an officer, so noble-hearted a patriot."[239] Concluding this final act of friendship, Russell saw the body of his boyhood friend loaded on the cars for his final trip home to Lansing and the funeral for the fallen that awaited him.

On Sunday, October 12, 1862, the largest funeral ever held in the capital city was conducted. Lieutenant Whitman's remains lay in state in the House of Representatives in the old Lansing State Capitol, the only documented occurrence of a person lying in state there. The chambers were festooned with flags, the coffin covered with the stars and stripes and decorated with flowers and the military cap and sash of the deceased. He was attended by a military guard of the Third Michigan Infantry, commanded by Lieutenant Joseph Mason. Mason was home in the Lansing area on recruiting leave, recuperating from wounds received at the Battle of Fair Oaks, Virginia, earlier that spring. In January 1863, he accepted

The first Lansing capitol, where Lieutenant Whitman lay in state, was constructed in 1847. After the present capitol opened in 1879, the building was used as a factory and was consumed by fire in 1882. *Archives of Michigan.*

a captain's commission, and on May 3, he, too, was killed in action at the Battle of Chancellorsville, Virginia.[240]

Lieutenant Whitman's funeral sermon was preached by the Reverend Edward Meyer, rector of Lansing's St. Paul's Episcopal Church. Reverend Meyer had previously served as the chaplain for the First Michigan Three Months Infantry Regiment. Tragically, just one week prior, he held the funeral service for his own seventeen-year-old eldest son, Henry Meyer, who was also killed at Antietam fighting with Company F of the Seventeenth Michigan Volunteer Infantry. Henry had been buried on the field in a soldier's grave, his family most likely lacking the means to bring his body home.[241] William Jordan and Ephraim Meachum, Lansing boys fighting with the Seventeenth, were also killed in action at Antietam and South Mountain.

At Whitman's funeral, the solemn and impressive Masonic rites were performed, and the remains were taken to the place of interment, followed by a large concourse of citizens and by the fire companies in uniform and the Masons in full regalia. The military escort discharged its farewell shots over the grave "and the earth closed forever upon the mortal remains of the heroic and lamented Whitman."[242]

Company C of the First USSS was largely held in reserve, although under almost constant artillery fire, at the Battle of Antietam. On August 31, just prior to the battle, Lieutenant Baker received promotion to the rank of captain. In his letter of recommendation to Michigan governor Austin Blair, Baker's commanding officer stated he was a "brave and competent officer as he has proved it by his conduct in the field and the good management of his Company in camp and on the march."[243] The Lansing paper further reported, "This promotion has been well earned, by our gallant young townsman."[244] From the Battle of Antietam to the time the First and Second U.S. Sharpshooters were consolidated into one regiment in December 1864, the regiments fought in the majority of the same battles, including the Battle of Fredericksburg in December 1862 and the Mud March in January 1863.

In February 1863, Captain Baker received a short furlough and, while home, was presented with an officer's sword by his friends and supporters. In presenting the sword, Lansing mayor William H. Chapman stated Baker was well tried as a citizen, but many were unsure about his prospects as a soldier because he had no military experience—to wit, he was a true citizen-soldier. Chapman reported they followed the captain's actions with great anxiety, and he had proved himself "as a true and valiant American soldier, and well-earned the promotions....Take this sword, and whenever you may hereafter be; whether in the lonely tent, or amid the wild strife of the battle-field, rest assured that the prayers and best wishes of the donors with other of your fellow citizens will accompany you."[245] Baker replied that the honor was unexpected and it was with comingled feelings of joy and sorrow that he accepted the sword.

By May, Captain Baker was again with his regiment amid the Chancellorsville Campaign. At Chancellorsville, William Denny reported to the *Lansing State Republican*, "in the thickest of the fight the Sharpshooters particularly distinguished themselves."[246] Baker, while in command of sixty-five men from Companies C, I and K, captured 365 Confederates of the Twenty-Third Georgia Regiment. The company took heavy casualties, and many were wounded, including Lansing soldiers: Henry Ballard, James Dillabaugh, Henry Gilchrist and Captain Baker, who was slightly wounded in the left breast by a Confederate shell fragment.[247] This was in addition to the wound Baker had received to his left wrist the previous fall at the Second Battle of Bull Run. Nonetheless, by June, he had recovered and was on duty again with his regiment.[248]

July 2, 1863, found the Lansing Sharpshooters heavily engaged among the rocky ridges, orchards and fields near the crossroads town of Gettysburg,

Pennsylvania. Around eight o'clock in the morning on the second day of the battle, the Sharpshooters were ordered by General Dan Sickles to advance beyond the Union line in skirmish lines to the Peach Orchard to gauge enemy strength. Captain Baker, along with Company C and five other companies of sharpshooters, advanced beyond the Devil's Den and Little Round Top to the far extreme left of the Union line. There, they skirmished heavily with the enemy, and according to Lieutenant Colonel Casper Trepp of the First USSS, Baker's line of skirmishers were in front of the center of the Third Army Corps, and "he took his position without order, following the instincts of the true soldier.... When the enemy pushed his skirmish line to and across the road, he charged with part of his command on the enemy, driving them across the field. I have to call especial

Henry Ballard was twenty-two when he enlisted. He was wounded at Chancellorsville, transferred to the Invalid Corps and was discharged from the service in 1864. *Brian T. White Collection.*

attention to the good behavior of this officer in all the engagements, and I would respectfully recommend him for decoration or honorable mention."[249] Trepp's recommendation was for Baker to receive the Medal of Honor for the valor he displayed at Gettysburg, an honor never bestowed.

It has been debated by historians that General Sickles, by ordering these men forward, either put the left of the Union line in jeopardy or perhaps gave Confederate general James Longstreet pause in ordering an advance and therefore bought the time needed for the Union troops to reinforce Little Round Top. It was the opinion of the Sharpshooters that "but for their persistent determination to hold their ground, the enemy must have crossed the Emmitsburg road before our infantry were in position to check them."[250] Based on this assertion, it may be argued that Captain James Baker and the men of Lansing played a pivotal role in the final Union victory at Gettysburg, a victory that marked the beginning of the end of the Confederacy.

After General Lee's withdrawal from Gettysburg, the Union army followed in pursuit, albeit after suffering high losses in Pennsylvania. The pursuit was not as strenuous as President Lincoln would have preferred. On July 17, the Sharpshooters crossed the river at Harpers Ferry, marching along the base of the mountains by Snickers Gap and proceeding to Manassas Gap, where they again engaged the enemy in the Battle of Wapping Heights or Manassas Gap, Virginia, on July 23. The Sharpshooters were detailed as skirmishers during the fight and very early on expended their sixty rounds of ammunition per man, taking many casualties, including Captain Baker, who was wounded for the third time; this wounding would lead to his return to Lansing and his eventual discharge.

On recovering from his wounds after his honorable discharge, Baker formed a chair company with his brother Oscar, who also survived the war, later becoming the assistant superintendent and the acting superintendent of the State Reform School for Boys in Lansing. He worked as a detective, was elected sheriff, then worked in the lumber business in northern Michigan before returning to Lansing, where he passed away peacefully on August 3, 1909, at the age of sixty-nine.

The war, however, was far from over for the other Lansing men of the USSS. In early 1864, a large portion of the men having reenlisted, they were granted a thirty-day furlough home to Lansing. While there, they recruited heavily to fill their depleted ranks.[251] Company B had left Lansing in the fall of 1861 with 106 men and had seen action in fifteen battles and many skirmishes, being under fire a total of twenty-nine days. Two men had been killed in action, including John Skinner of Ingham County and J.J. Whitman of Lansing; fourteen men died from disease; and four were languishing in Southern prisons. Twenty-four of the forty-two remaining members reenlisted, and nine new Lansing recruits joined them. Among the new Lansing recruits was Charles Hunt. "Charley" was known and beloved by many in Lansing due to his work in the post office, the state treasury department and the Middle Town banking office of J.C. Bailey and Company. According to the *Republican*, "Although a Democrat, [he] has always been patriotically inclined and has finally concluded to give his personal service towards finishing the war."[252]

The spring and summer of 1864 found the USSS engaged in General Grant's Overland Campaign, and the weekly Lansing paper included growing casualty lists. In a letter to the paper dated June 1, Captain Adolphus Guest, who had enlisted in New York City but had familial ties to Lansing, reported the Company B casualties: At the Battle of Spotsylvania, Virginia, in May: Benjamin Goodhue, who had been a farmer in the First Ward, wounded in the chest and later discharged; Wilber Howard, who had worked as a dry goods clerk in Coryell's Middle Town store, wounded in the left arm; Albert Hulsapple, a laborer in the First Ward, wounded in the face; John Bohnet, severe mortal wound to right leg.[253]

Left: Captain Adolphus Guest, Second U.S. Sharpshooters, Company B. *Brian T. White Collection.*

Right: Carte de visite, or calling card, of Adolphus A. Guest. *Archives of Michigan.*

By June, the Lansing companies were engaged in the battles and eventual long-term siege of Petersburg, Virginia, and there Corporal William Sherwood was wounded, as was Henry Parker, both of Lansing. Charley Hunt was listed as missing in action, presumed captured. He was eventually paroled by the Confederates but, on his journey home, died of disease in Annapolis, Maryland. Also captured on June 21 during the Battle of Jerusalem Plank Road was John Ellis; he was twenty-two, had lived in Lansing's First Ward and was working as a cabinetmaker when he and his brother Thomas, age twenty, mustered in as new recruits with Company B. It was later determined that John died at the infamous Confederate prison at Andersonville, Georgia.[254] Another brother, George, had been killed at the Second Battle of Bull Run fighting with Company G of the Third Infantry. By August, Company B could only muster twenty-one guns.[255] Tragedy was not limited to the ranks of soldiers and often struck home while the men were away at war. David Ward, the thirteen-year-old son of Company B sharpshooter Ulysses Ward, was riding on the plank road just east of Lansing when he was thrown by his horse, suffering a fatal brain injury[256] and leaving his mother Laura to cope with the absence of her husband and the premature death of her son.

As the armies settled into trench and siege warfare outside of Petersburg, a precursor to the trench warfare of World War I, a soldier-correspondent from the Sharpshooters wrote home that the men were exchanging coffee with the rebels for Southern tobacco, also stating, "You at home cannot desire peace any more than we, but we are not enough desirous of it to give the South their independence. We are anxious to get home, but we will fight to the last before we will do that."[257] By November, the men were building winter shelters and voting in the 1864 presidential election, the Michigan state authorities having sent voting commissioners into the field to ensure the soldiers' votes were counted. This action helped insure Lincoln's election victory over his Democratic challenger, former Union general George B. McClellan.

The plight of the besieged Confederate forces at Petersburg was apparent; one of the Sharpshooters recorded the rebs were picking up spent Union bullets for reuse, stating the firing was so severe a man collecting one-ounce spent bullets could "pick up twenty pounds in less than one hour."[258] The Sharpshooters were also foraging for supplies and food. During one of the numerous battles of the Weldon Railroad in December, a Lansing soldier reported: "We had orders to halt half an hour for coffee. Just then a nice pig came running through the ranks. He was knocked over by one man, stuck by a second, skinned by a third and fourth, while a fifth ran for water and a sixth for wood, and in this way our supper was soon under full headway.… In twenty-five minutes the pig was alive, killed and eaten."[259]

In February 1865, their ranks severely depleted, the Sharpshooters, which had already been consolidated into one regiment, were disbanded, and the companies were attached to regiments from their respective states. The few remaining Michigan men were reassigned to the Fifth Michigan Infantry and fought with them until Lee's surrender at Appomattox and their eventual muster out on July 5, 1865, at Jeffersonville, Indiana.

The *Lansing State Republican*, on May 3, 1865, printed the statistics for the Second USSS, and according to the article, the regiment fought in twenty-two battles and fifty-four skirmishes, from its first action at Falmouth, Virginia, on May 19, 1862, to its last action at Hatchers Run, Virginia, on February 5, 1865. Total enlistment was 1,182, with 530 men killed or wounded; when it was disbanded, the regiment mustered only 170 men. On July 12, the paper reported the upcoming return of the few remaining Lansing soldiers, "They went out from us: they went out for us: let us all unite in doing honor to our returning heroes."[260]

Chapter 8

LET THOSE SCARS BE AN HONOR TO YOU

The Eighth Michigan Volunteer Infantry Regiment, Elder Zouaves, Company E

I n June 1861, a unique company of men formed under the command of Lansing citizen Matthew Elder.[261] The volunteers of Company E of the Eighth Michigan Infantry were inspired by the French Algerian troops and the military tactics and uniforms of the north African Zouazoua tribe. The Zouave craze hit American military organizations in the late 1850s, and when the war started, numerous companies and regiments adopted the truly unusual uniforms of the Zouaves. The Zouave uniform, with many variations, usually consisted of baggy red pantaloon pants, a short blue shell jacket with red piping, a sleeveless vest, white gaiters and a turban with a red fez. As the war progressed, the impracticality of the ensemble led many of the units to abandon it in favor of the more practical and easily procured standard uniform.

The captain and namesake of Company E was Matthew Elder. Elder was born in Richland County, Ohio, and served in the Mexican-American War from 1846 to 1847 as a sergeant with the Third Ohio Infantry Regiment.[262] After his return from the war, he married Calista (also known as Celestia) Baker, and the young family, which would eventually include five children, moved to Lansing in the early 1850s. Elder was a Second Ward alderman, inventor, architect and master carpenter. In 1858, he designed and oversaw the construction of the second Ingham County Courthouse (1858–1904), "an imposing brick structure" in Mason, Michigan.[263] "Captain Elder may be relied upon as the right kind of man....He has seen service in Mexico and is a man who will look well to the comfort of his men and will not desert

Right: Unidentified Zouave soldier, Eighth Michigan Volunteer Infantry Regiment, Company E of Lansing, as identified on the kepi on the table. *Dan Miller Collection*.

Below: The 1858 Ingham County Courthouse in Mason, Michigan, was designed by Matthew Elder, who also oversaw the construction of the building. *Geil, Harley and Siverd, Library of Congress, Geography and Map Division*.

Ingham Co. Court House, Mason

them in the hour of danger."[264] Elder's younger brother John A. Elder would also sign the muster sheet for Company E and by war's end would advance to the rank of captain.

The first lieutenant was thirty-five-year-old Abraham Cottrell, who emigrated from Birmingham, England, and settled in Lansing as a young man. Cottrell worked as a gunsmith, but he also operated a Middle Town photography studio in partnership with Phillip Engelhart.[265] Second Lieutenant Nelson C. Chapman, a Second Ward carpenter/joiner, was with his regiment through the first year of service and was then honorably discharged. Former Lansing resident Reverend William Mahon of Northville was appointed regimental chaplain.

The regimental surgeon was Dr. Hulbert Shank. Dr. Shank moved to Lansing in 1848 from New York State and established a practice in Middle Town, while serving as the first physician to the Boys' Reform School. Shank was an active member of the Lansing Republican Club and the Capitol Lodge of Strict Observance No. 66 F&AM of the Masons. In November 1860, he was elected as the Ingham County state representative but would miss most of the sessions of the twenty-first legislature after accepting his appointment, in August 1861, as surgeon of the Eighth Michigan Infantry Regiment.

Shank's son, Rush Jesse Shank, who was one of the first pioneer children born in Lansing in 1848, would also enlist, at age sixteen, along with many of his classmates from the New York Oakwood Academy. He served in the 148th New York Infantry, survived the war, declined his appointment to West Point and instead received his medical degree from the University of Michigan. Dr. Rush Shank followed in his father's footsteps, practicing medicine in Lansing while serving as the first commander of the Charles T. Foster Post of the Grand Army of the Republic and as state commander of the GAR.[266]

Among the enlisted men were the Baldwin brothers: Timothy, age twenty-two; Franklin, age twenty-three; and Samuel, age twenty-eight, "all going together to fight for their country."[267] The Baldwin brothers would see service with the Eighth and Twentieth Michigan Infantry Regiments and would each advance in rank to noncommissioned and commissioned officer status, with Samuel leading Company E as its captain in the last year of the war.[268] Soldiers from many of Lansing's notable founding families were among the ranks of the Eighth, including Martin Beebe, Henry Buck, Sibley Ingersoll and Edgar Shattuck.

Above, left: Dr. Hulbert Shank, surgeon of the Eighth Michigan Infantry Regiment. *Collection of Craig Whitford.*

Above, right: Rush Jesse Shank enlisted and fought with a New York regiment, studied medicine at the University of Michigan and then opened a medical practice in Lansing. *Collection of Craig Whitford.*

Left: Edgar Shattuck was twenty-one when he enlisted and fought with the Eighth Michigan in the last year of the war. His father and three brothers also enlisted with other Lansing units. *Archives of Michigan.*

The day before his company's departure from Lansing, Captain Elder wrote a letter to his friend David Bagley. Bagley, who was a friend and correspondent to many Lansing soldiers, was a clerk in the auditor general's office and a contributing editor of the *Republican* and owned a small fruit orchard in Lansing.[269] Elder, seeking the protection of his family if he should fall in battle, wrote:

> *Sir you are a man which I consider my neighbour…and one who I Shall ever remember while my light holds out to elumin this tentament of Clay….
> And in the care of my God & the Protection of Such as you I leave my wife
> & Little ones hoping & trusting in that God who never as yet has forsaken
> the just & true…hoping that I may by the grace of God be permitted to
> return to my familey & friends to enjoy the fruits of a Peacefull & happy
> Country with you & mine, your friend M. Elder.[270]*

At 5:45 a.m. on Friday, August 23, 1861, forty-six members of the Elder Zouaves formed in front of the Benton House in Upper Town and were escorted by the fire department to the corner of Washington and Michigan Avenues. On the steps of the Bailey Banking Office, "a valuable pistol was presented to Capt. Elder on behalf of the citizens of Lansing"[271] by his friend and confidant D.M. Bagley. In presenting the pistol, Bagley stated: "Captain Elder…you are about to leave us to command a noble and gallant band of volunteers, and we desire in this public manner, to testify our esteem for you as a neighbor, friend and patriot.…We earnestly hope, when peace… shall again bless our now distracted land, that you may be safely restored to your home and friends." Captain Elder responded: "The time for speech-making is past. This is a time for action.…I will strive to discharge my whole duty, endeavoring to do honor both to the givers and the recipient of this token.…Fellow soldiers…let us greet our friends with three good cheers, and fall into line."[272] The company then boarded the assembled wagons for St. Johns, where they were graciously greeted and fed dinner before boarding the train to Grand Rapids, where they would join the other companies of the Eighth Infantry.

By September 4, the last squad of new recruits for Company E had left Lansing for Grand Rapids, reaching the one-hundred-man capacity of the company. The evening before their departure for Detroit, they were feted by the ladies of Grand Rapids with a "bountiful table, furnished with every kind of delicacy."[273] The regiment left Detroit's Fort Wayne on September 27, arriving in D.C. on the thirtieth, and went into camp on Meridian Hill.

VANDERBILT-

The *Vanderbilt* was donated by the wealthy American industrialist Cornelius Vanderbilt, who made his fortune in railroads and shipping. Sketch by Civil War artist Alfred Waud. *Library of Congress.*

On October 19, it boarded the steamship *Vanderbilt* and on November 8 landed at Hilton Head and then continued on to Beaufort and Brickyard Point on the Coosaw River in South Carolina. It was on the Coosaw River that the Eighth first engaged the enemy. In a letter to his wife, Elder stated that the rebels fought hard, showing "good blood for a bad cause."[274] Lieutenant Cottrell was cited for bravery by Brigadier General Isaac Stevens while leading an assault against a Confederate battery. Shortly after, Cottrell was made Stevens's aide-de-camp. Cottrell was later badly injured when his horse fell on him and fractured his right shoulder; the injury caused him pain for the rest of his life. Cottrell eventually asked to be relieved from his post as aide to Stevens and returned to command of his company.[275]

Company E had lost no men in combat, but despite the efforts of surgeon Shank, several succumbed to disease, including John Hall, Cornelius Haviland, Lyman Hull, Wilbert Palmenter and Thomas Perry. Dr. Shank likewise had to resign his commission due to ill health and was honorably discharged from the service on January 13. Shank returned to Lansing and served as the examining surgeon for the Third District draft board, a member of the Reform School Board of Control and president of the Lansing Board of Education and the State Medical Society.[276] In 1866, he partnered in medical practice with fellow former regimental surgeon Dr.

George Ranney, who had recently settled in Lansing. Dr. Ranney, surgeon of the Second Michigan Cavalry Regiment, was the recipient of the Medal of Honor for most distinguished gallantry, at great personal risk aiding a wounded soldier at the Battle of Resaca, Georgia, in 1864. Ranney Park on the east side of Lansing, the property for which was donated by Ranney, bears his name.

Historians debate if Michigan and Union soldiers fought to uphold the Constitution and put down a rebellion or to end slavery. Many Lansing citizens and soldiers did not hide their feelings about the cause of the war, as was the case with Tillinghast Brownell, serving with the Twentieth Michigan Infantry. In a letter to David Bagley, Brownell wrote that our country "has been cursed nearly four years by the cruelest and most causeless rebellion… which has caused rivers of our best blood…and filled the land with Widows, Orphans, Cripples and desolate hearthstones and all this has been done to Sustain that relick of barbarism Human Slavery."[277] However, another of Bagley's friends, Captain Matt Elder, in a letter to his uncle, Harvey Baker, expressed a very different opinion: "All I want to see accomplished by this war is that the Rebels lay down their armes and return to their allegiances to the Constitution of our fathers without the alteration of one single word therein then I will strike hands with them"[278]—very different sentiments of men from the same city, with the same circle of friends.

On April 16, 1862, seven companies of the Eighth Regiment were landed on Wilmington Island, Georgia, and there again engaged the rebels with a loss of eleven killed and thirty-four wounded, none from Company E. Shortly after the battle, Captain Elder was sent home to Lansing on a twenty-day furlough. In reporting on his homecoming, the *Republican* stated, "The children moved immediately upon his works and carried them gallantly by storm. The vanquished captain yielded himself a prisoner, delivered up his sword to his second son upon demand and was marched into the custody of his rejoicing wife."[279] While home on leave, Captain Elder was discharged from the Eighth in order to accept a commission as a lieutenant in the Eleventh U.S. Infantry.

Company E, under the command of Lieutenant Cottrell, saw action again in the Battle of Secessionville, James Island, southwest of the city of Charleston, South Carolina, on June 16, 1862. The Eighth suffered large losses, including Lieutenant Cottrell, who was severely wounded leading another charge against a Confederate battery. It was originally believed Cottrell had been killed in action, but while he was grievously wounded in the side and back, he would recover, albeit in the dubious care of the

Abraham Cottrell was a photographer in Lansing when he was commissioned as a first lieutenant in Company E. He was captured at the battle of James Island, and after his release, he resumed service and mustered out of the Veteran Reserve Corps at the end of the war. *Archives of Michigan.*

Confederates. Lieutenant Cottrell would see the inside of three Confederate prisoner of war camps before being paroled and eventually making his way back to his regiment.[280] The *Republican* told all too well the tale of the union losses at Secessionville: "Michigan has met a serious loss in the slaughter of the Michigan Eighth at Secessionville….It now appears this was almost a wanton sacrifice of life."[281] Frederick Turrell was killed, and the wounded included Lansing enlistees: Henry Chadwick, Edward Light, Heman Throop and George Truce. Turrell's younger brother Charles was also in the fight. The Turrell brothers enlisted together in Lansing, but their farm was in Williamston. The Eighth suffered thirteen killed, ninety-eight wounded, thirty-five taken prisoner and thirty-six missing—assumed dead or prisoners.[282] On July 13, the regiment boarded transports and sailed for Fortress Monroe and Virginia; they were then engaged in the Battles of Second Bull Run, Chantilly, South Mountain and Antietam.

In dire need of new enlistees to fill the ranks of those killed, wounded, disabled or captured, several officers were sent home on recruiting missions. In Lansing, the recruiting office for the Eighth was in the Edgar House. With the losses suffered in the officers' ranks at the Battle of James Island, promotions were awarded to several Lansing soldiers. Lieutenant Cottrell, after his release, was promoted to captain, Second Lieutenant N.C. Chapman to first lieutenant and George "Whit" Chandler to first lieutenant. Prior to the war, Chandler worked as a dry goods clerk in Charles Seymour's Lower Town store. The ranks were further depleted by the loss of many men from disease, death or disability discharge, including Lansing soldiers Martin Beebe, Henry Buck, Edwin Benson, John Burgoyne, Dorman Fuller, John Fuller, Thomas Little, who was a drummer, and Daniel Stafford, principal regimental musician. In October, Lieutenant Elder returned to Lansing once more, this time to recruit for the Eleventh U.S. Infantry. By December 1862, just before the Battle of

Fredericksburg, only "about thirty men of Captain Elder's Company E, which was organized in Lansing, still remain in the field."[283]

Earning their nomenclature "The Wandering Regiment," the Eighth was sent to the Western Theater of the war early in 1863. Captain Cottrell was forced to resign due to his failing health on March 19, 1863, although he would later serve to great effect in the Invalid or Veteran Reserve Corps before returning to Lansing and his photography studio.[284] A resolution honoring Cottrell, issued by Company E from its camp in Lebanon, Kentucky, stated, "We recognize in Capt. Cottrell a true soldier and a brave man."[285] In April, John Elder followed in his older brother's footsteps as he accepted a promotion to first lieutenant of Company E, and by May, the regiment was engaged in rebuilding and guarding a bridge on the Green River near Lebanon, Kentucky. From this camp, an "Old Soldier" wrote to the *Republican*, "Many a brother or dear comrade has fallen by our sides.… Still our love for the Union is as pure as it was when we left our Peninsular State."[286] From June 22 to July 4, the Eighth participated in the Siege of Vicksburg, Mississippi.

While his namesake, the Elder Zouaves, was encamped outside of Vicksburg, Lieutenant Matt Elder was fighting with the Eleventh U.S. Infantry amid the boulders of the Valley of Death between the Devil's Den and the Wheatfield at the Battle of Gettysburg. In the fight on July 2, fifteen of the twenty-five officers of the Eleventh were killed or wounded. Elder was severely wounded in the left leg and was assisted to relative safety behind a large boulder amid the ongoing fight. Seeking shelter behind the boulder were several other wounded Union soldiers. Rebel sharpshooters spotted the men and started picking them off one by one. The position was retaken by Union troops, and the grievously wounded Lieutenant Elder was taken to a field hospital. The amputation of his leg above the knee was necessary, and three days later, word was received by his family that his life was in severe jeopardy. Lieutenant Matthew Elder, inventor, builder, husband and father of five, died as a result of his injuries on July 25.[287] Elder's body was embalmed and shipped home to Lansing; the funeral service was held at his residence. He was interred, with his Masonic brethren conducting the rights, on August 2. "He leaves a family and a large circle of friends to mourn his loss and his name is added to the long list of those who died for their country."[288]

In the fall of 1863, Lieutenant John Elder, who came home attempting to entice recruits for his company before the January draft, reported that of 112 men of Company E, 64 had been lost to death or discharge. Among

Right: Captain John Elder. *Archives of Michigan.*

Below: Boulder at the Devil's Den at Gettysburg, where Lieutenant Matt Elder sought shelter after his wounding. *Photo courtesy of the National Park Service, Gettysburg National Military Park.*

the dead was Sibley Ingersoll: he died of disease of the lungs, he was only eighteen when he enlisted and he was the eldest of eight children. The Ingersolls were respected Lansing-area farmers. Sibley was in the regimental drum corps, and Lieutenant Colonel Ralph Ely personally wrote the letter of condolence to the *Republican*: "He died a worthy, willing and obedient soldier."[289] In early 1864, the regiment returned to Michigan for a thirty-day furlough as Veteran Volunteers after the majority of the men reenlisted for another three years or the duration of the war. After their coveted and well-deserved furlough home, the Eighth was again attached to the Army of the Potomac and would finish the war fighting in the Eastern Theater.

Among the new Company E recruits was twenty-two-year-old Edward West Flower of Lansing. Born in Brooklyn, New York, Flower moved to Lansing, where he was working as a clerk. In his year of service, Flower sent numerous reports and letters back to the *Republican*. In a letter dated April 19, 1864, he reported they were encamped "in a very pleasant place....We have not yet had a chance since the return of the regiment to try our fighting qualities....We shall have the opportunity of showing the enemies...the kind of stuff Michigan boys are made of."[290] Less than one month later, Flower's enthusiasm for fighting would be satiated in the Overland Campaign and in the tangled undergrowth of the Wilderness.

In a letter to his parents dated May 10 and subsequently published in *The Republican*, Flower wrote of the carnage and brutality of war.

> *I expect you are getting more than anxious to hear from me....I am lying in a rifle pit, behind breast works...with the shells from the batteries of both our own and the rebels, passing over our heads....We have had a very severe and trying time....No one but those who actually experience the perils and sufferings of the battle field can imagine the reality of it....It seems like nothing else than God's merciful Providence that I have been preserved.... The old soldiers say it was the worst battle they were ever in....I feel lonesome enough here now. Of all the boys that came with me I am the only one left.*[291]

Private Flower continued the letter to his parents:

> *We arose up with a yell and drove the fleeing regiment back again...when suddenly a force five to our one, rose up and charged on us....From then until sun-down it seemed as if the bullets came in perfect showers....I had*

hardly the strength to load. The sweat rolled off of me, and the smoke and powder blinded me....Davenport, fell dead by my side, another one severely wounded behind me, and others falling around, I felt sick....we lost our Colonel [Frank Graves] *together with two captains and about fifty privates killed and missing, and 100 wounded....Pray daily for me, that whatever befalls me, I may be ready for the issue.*[292]

In a report to the *Republican*, Lieutenant Elder noted the losses of the Eighth and Company E: Nathan Everett and Matthew Fitzpatrick were killed, Andrew Vanheuven was wounded, Andrew Deitz was missing. Fitzpatrick was captured, only to die in captivity three months later at the infamous Andersonville prison. Two days after sending his report, Lieutenant Elder, James Gordon and Daniel Wiser were wounded, and Elisha Herrington and Farrell Cowley were killed at the Battle of Spotsylvania on May 12. Edward Flower was also wounded, shot in the right foot, his injury requiring the amputation of the foot and his discharge. Flower eventually returned to Lansing after convalescing, and in 1870, he was working as a clerk in the auditor general's department at the Lansing capitol. Answering a different call, Flower was ordained an Episcopalian priest and, along with his wife Jaen and their children, ministered a parish in St. Joseph, Missouri. He also served in numerous capacities in the Missouri Grand Army of the Republic, including that of state chaplain. When Flower died in 1911 and was buried in St. Joseph, his wish was that he be buried not in his Union army uniform but in his priestly vestments.[293]

The fighting continued between the Armies of the Potomac and Northern Virginia, as the casualty numbers on both sides continued to rise, including many Lansing men: Franklin Burnham, wounded in June at Cold Harbor; Robert Fulton, killed in action at Petersburg; Judson Painly and Peter Portney, both only eighteen and two months in the service, wounded at Petersburg, along with George Truce the following day. In August, Wesley McCave was taken prisoner at the Battle of Weldon Railroad, and John Davidson was wounded.

In August, Lieutenant John Elder was again in Lansing, recovering from his wounds and recruiting for the Eighth, with his recruiting station in the Middle Town bookstore of William Carr. "The Eighth has a reputation second to no other regiment in the field....While he [Elder] would prefer recruits to enter his own regiment, he will enlist men for any of the old regiments."[294] By the fall, Elder returned to the front lines in the southwest trenches surrounding Petersburg, Virginia, and reported in a letter penned

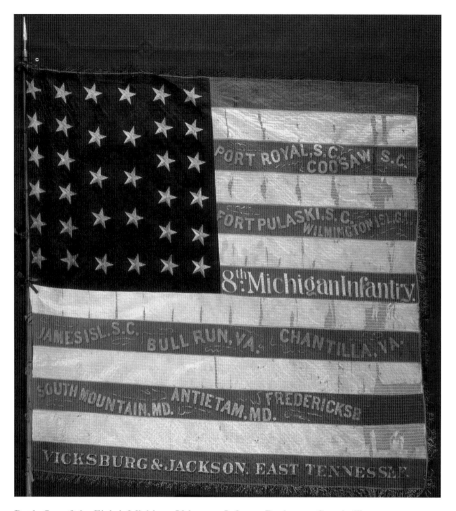

Battle flag of the Eighth Michigan Volunteer Infantry Regiment. *Save the Flags.*

on Thanksgiving, "The boys that are with us feel well....When a charge is ordered, the boys go in with a yell, regardless of the past or future, let the consequences be what they may....They are no cowards."[295]

The following spring, the Eighth Michigan would be among the first Union troops into the captured Confederate stronghold of Petersburg. On August 12, 1865, several months after Lee's surrender at Appomattox, the few surviving members were mustered out of the service at Delaney House in D.C. and returned home. That fall, Captain John Elder married Ellen Moon of DeWitt in a double marriage ceremony in which his sister Barbara married Robert Godfrey, also a recently returned veteran. Elder spent the rest of his life in Lansing and owned a mitten and glove store across from the old capitol; he died in 1889 at age fifty-three.

In his final report to the *Republican*, Captain Elder listed the statistics for the Lansing company. Of the 168 men, the majority from Lansing, 73 were discharged for wounds and disabilities, 16 were killed in action, 26 died of disease and wounds, 11 were transferred to Invalid Corps and only 35 men mustered out with Captain Elder. In addressing his men, Elder wrote:

> *After four years of war, carnage and bloodshed you, a few, are permitted to return to your respective homes, there to enjoy that peaceful bliss, which none but a soldier can fully appreciate….By your patriotic devotion…you have obliterated every vestige of that cursed institution—slavery….You left your homes, your firesides, your wives, your families and those most dear and near to you and volunteered….Well have you done your duty….There are but few among you whose persons do not show the marks of rebel missiles, let those scars be an honor to you….I bid you an affectionate farewell.*[296]

Chapter 9

THE MICHIGAN FEMALE COLLEGE

The Rogers Sisters Start a College

Duringthe fourteen years of its existence, the Michigan Female College was to Lansing a recognized social and education power, whose far reaching influence it is not easy to estimate."[297] Some of the men fighting with the Lansing-based companies left younger sisters behind who were likewise toiling to improve their country and city by becoming educated, informed citizens. In 1855, on the outskirts of Lansing's Lower Town, the Michigan Female College was established. The college sprang from the inspiration and support of many individuals, including notable Lansing residents Daniel Case, A.N. Hart, H.H. Smith and James Turner, but owed its existence and success primarily to Abigail and Delia Rogers. Under the leadership of the Rogers sisters, the college would eventually have over one thousand pupils pass through its rigorous classical and scientific curriculum from 1855 to 1869. In the early days of the college, these students also included boys, some of whom would see action in the Civil War with Lansing-based companies. In 1869, the college closed after the untimely death of Abigail Rogers, with the campus eventually becoming the site for the Michigan School for the Blind. The formative years of the Michigan Female College were, however, amidst the uncertainty and ravages of the Civil War.

The Female College was established after it became apparent the Michigan University in Ann Arbor and the recently created Michigan Agricultural College in East Lansing would not admit female students and the state legislature failed to act upon the issue. "The state having made such liberal provision for her sons, was guilty of great injustice in withholding the same advantage from those equally her wards and children."[298] Perhaps with a tinge of guilt, the state legislature permitted the Female College to hold daily instruction in the chambers of the state capitol for the first two years and then permitted the college to conduct large meetings and graduation ceremonies in the building. A twenty-acre parcel of land was donated to the college by a benefactor, and the *Republican* reported that "the location of the college is an exceedingly pleasant one."[299] The school secured $20,000 in subscriptions. By the fall of 1858, a wing of the central building was completed under the capable supervision of Abigail Rogers. Having expended the full subscription in constructing one wing of what was envisioned to be a central and multi-winged building, "the ladies of Lansing came together, and by the pleasant lightening of labor made by many hands fitted and sewed the carpets for all the rooms in the building."[300]

Abigail Rogers was born in Avon, New York, in 1818 and after receiving her formal education, served in numerous capacities in the field of education. Her positions included preceptress of White Plains Seminary in Westchester County, New York; head of the female department of the Genesee Wesleyan Seminary in Lima, New York; head of the female department at Albion, Michigan; and preceptress of the State Normal School (Eastern Michigan University) in Ypsilanti, Michigan—then on to Lansing, joined by her sister Delia.[301]

The Michigan Female College. *Library of Congress, Geography and Map Division.*

In the early summer of 1861, while Lansing's young men were answering the call to arms, the college held commencement exercises for its first full graduating class of eleven young ladies, at this point having become largely self-sustaining.[302] Eighty students were in attendance, with thirty-five boarding at the college and the remainder with the citizens of Lansing. According to the *Lansing State Republican*, "The boarding school seemed like a well-regulated Christian family, the accomplished instructors are surrounded by affectionate and obedient daughters. The curriculum includes both a scientific and classical course."[303] Additional courses included arithmetic, grammar,

Abigail Rogers. *Archives of Michigan.*

reading, rhetoric, French, Latin, German, Greek, geology, botany, astronomy, logic, history and moral philosophy.

Commencements were preceded by a full week of public review of the students' abilities in examination exercises frequently held in the chambers of the state capitol. "The examinations evinced thoroughness of instruction and diligence and capacity on the part of the students. Almost every question, whether by teachers or visitors, within or without the textbooks, was satisfactorily answered."[304] The graduation ceremonies were well attended, with the Amboy, Lansing and Traverse Bay Railroad offering half-price fares for those attending. The ceremony included student recitations of original compositions on such topics as architecture and "civilization and the pulpit," interspersed with vocal and instrumental pieces and offerings by the Calliopean Society of the college.

The war, however, was never far from the thoughts and actions of the students of the college and "was a subject of frequent reference, but always of the expression of genuine feeling."[305] In sending receipt of a draft of seventy dollars donated by the college to the Michigan Relief Association, President J.M. Edmonds wrote: "The chronicles of these times will note, that while our university for young men has been so largely represented in all the battles for the Union; the young ladies of the Female College have no less manifested their spirit and patriotism in generous contributions to relieve the hardships and sufferings of our brave soldiers."[306]

Chapter 10

TO THE TENTED FIELD

The Twelfth Michigan Volunteer Infantry Regiment, Company G

T he Twelfth Michigan Volunteer Infantry Regiment organized at Niles, Michigan, in the late fall of 1861 and was mustered into federal service on March 5, 1862. On a snowy day in February, the regiment formed a hollow square on a frozen parade ground and a double sleigh appeared, drawn by two spirited black horses. It halted in the middle of the square, and Mary Penrose stood up in the sleigh to present the regiment with a "valuable silk banner" on behalf of the ladies of Niles. One of the ladies, Julia Bretschneider, whose husband, Robert, was a captain in the Second Michigan and later in the Twelfth Infantry, hand-sewed the flag and embroidered on it the motto "Michigan Expects every man to do his Duty."[307]

Witnessing this inspiring presentation were the men of Company G of the Twelfth Infantry, many of whom had just recently left their homes and loved ones in Lansing. The company was organized and commanded by the newly commissioned Captain Isaac M. Cravath, the thirty-five-year-old editor of the *Lansing State Republican*. In announcing his resignation from the paper, Cravath wrote: "I cannot longer refuse to listen to the voice of our country calling from a hundred battle fields for help."[308] In his last editorial, he encouraged the men of Lansing to enlist in his company. "Men, between the ages of eighteen and forty-five, of temperate habits, who love their country, and would put forth their hands to save it from destruction....No cause more glorious or more important ever presented itself for men to fight for than the preservation of the Union....Buckle on your armor and go with me to the tented field."[309]

Presentation battle flag of the Twelfth Michigan Volunteer Infantry Regiment. *Save the Flags.*

New York–born Cravath moved to Lansing around 1855 from Washtenaw County, Michigan, and at the outbreak of the war was living in the Third Ward with his newly wed wife, Elmira.[310] The first lieutenant of Company G was thirty-one-year-old George H. Gassimere (also known as Gassenmere). Gassimere was born in Baden, Germany, and was a carpenter-joiner in Lansing's First Ward. He left behind his wife, Susan, and three young children, all under the age of five. Among the other Lansing noncommissioned officers were Corporal Jerome Lafferty, a Lansing Township carpenter who left behind his eighteen-year-old bride, Almira; Corporal Thomas Kenyon; and Sergeant Henry C. Guest, who was a printer in the office of the *Lansing State Republican* and likewise left behind a new bride and young child.[311]

Another notable recruit, who enlisted in Lansing but was living in Vermontville with his wife, Harriet, and three young sons, was thirty-seven-year-old Dr. Robert C. Kedzie. He enlisted as the regimental assistant surgeon, and by the following year, he was commissioned the regimental surgeon.[312] Dr. Kedzie was in the first graduating class of the medical department at the University of Michigan in 1851. After the war, he served for forty years as a distinguished professor of chemistry at the Michigan Agricultural College.

Recruiting for Company G—"Cravath's Tigers," as they were known—continued through the fall of 1861, with recruiting offices in the Benton House, the office of the paper and A.W. Williams's Jewelry Store. As the men enlisted, Cravath escorted them to the Niles training camp. It appeared, from the recruiting advertisements, that they were headed not for war but for an all-expenses-paid trip to some exotic port. The advertisements exclaimed that Niles was "one of the most pleasant towns in the state....The quarters provided for the Regiment are of the most comfortable...with satisfactory provisions....This Regiment will probably go to Kentucky—a very healthy region of the country and most desirable point of destination."[313]

In late January 1862, Captain Cravath was the recipient, by way of numerous Lansing friends and associates, of a draft of thirty-five dollars, from which he was to purchase an officer's sash and sword. In thanking the donors, Cravath stated: "The patriotic citizens of Lansing have given repeated evidence of their zeal in behalf of the sustaining of the Government....Her men and money have been freely given for the preservation of the sacred trust of national existence."[314] He also reported that "all the boys of the Lansing Company are in good health and spirits and ready and anxious for service."[315]

The regiment left Camp Barker in Niles on March 19, 1862, on a twenty-eight car train, "with a sea of flashing bayonets, the colors flying and the bands playing...[and] the sad reflection that in all probability many of us would never return."[316] The train, stopping infrequently, went through Chicago, the Illinois prairies, Joliet, Peoria and Springfield and finally arrived at the Mississippi, with the men so crowded they were not able to sit or lie down during the twenty-four-hour trip. The men boarded a steamer to St. Louis, then a second steamer to Cairo, Illinois, and then proceeded on the Ohio River to Paducah, Kentucky, and the mouth of the Tennessee River. They boarded the steamer *The Luminary* and went up the Tennessee River, disembarking near an old steamboat stop "containing only a brick house, two shanties and a whiskey shop"[317] close to an old Methodist meeting house called Shiloh—an Old Testament name meaning "place of peace."[318]

General Ulysses S. Grant, fresh from his victories at Forts Henry and Donelson, sought to use his position at Pittsburg Landing/Shiloh to consolidate his forces with those of Union general Don Carlos Buell. This was in preparation for movement against Confederate forces under General Albert Sidney Johnston, then near the important railroad hub of Corinth, Mississippi. "To keep his men tough and nimble, Grant again made the fateful decision not to have them grab spades and dig entrenchments. He did not expect to stay long in the area."[319] A few days after arriving at Pittsburg Landing, the Twelfth was marched about three miles and set up camp at the "front and centerline of our army....Our camp was located in the timber on a very pleasant piece of ground near a spring that afforded us good water.... We pitched our tents and again resumed our camp life."[320]

At six o'clock on Sunday morning, April 6, 1862, the rebels attacked, while many of the Union soldiers were still asleep in their tents. A small detachment of the Twelfth had gone out to reconnoiter their front, under the command of Lieutenant Colonel Graves, the lieutenant having had a sense of foreboding about an impending attack, and they ran directly into the Confederate force, some forty-five thousand strong. Among the first shots fired in the Battle of Pittsburg Landing were those fired by men of the Twelfth Michigan Infantry, including Lansing's Company G. "No spot upon the whole field bore such terrible evidence of carnage as that in front of the position taken by the Michigan Twelfth...in a space of not over three acres of ground four hundred rebels left dead upon the field....Bodies lay so close upon each other, that one could have walked over nearly the whole space upon them alone."[321] "The bucolic setting, with its gently rolling woods and scattered meadows, soon became a charnel house....Bodies of soldiers piled up in heaps....Shiloh was a free-for-all of death."[322]

According to an article published in the *Republican*, "The Lansing Company with two other companies were the first companies in the fight, and that they actually brought on the battle."[323] The article, paying homage to Company G's nomenclature, stated they fought like "so many tigers" and Captain Cravath was in the "hottest of the fight during the entire two days, cool and undaunted, cheering his men on to the conflict. Ingham County may well be proud of such a hero."[324]

The April 30 edition of the *Republican* told all too well the tale of woe visited upon the city with its casualty list from Shiloh. Private John Schleicher, age nineteen, was killed in action. Private David Schaible, a First Ward carpenter born in Württemberg, Germany, was wounded. Corporal Jerome B. Lafferty was taken prisoner; he was later paroled, died on the way home at Washington, D.C., and was buried at the Soldiers Home. John Nagel was captured. William Oatley, who had enlisted on Christmas Day the previous year, was also captured—he would later die in the Confederate prison pen at Camp Oglethorpe, Macon, Georgia, never to see another Lansing Christmas. Corporal Thomas Kenyon was listed as missing in action. In 1863, after spending six and a half months as a guest of the Confederacy, Kenyon was paroled and came home to Lansing, reporting on the horrendous conditions of the Confederate prisons. "It was evidently the intention of the rebels to kill their prisoners by starvation…for over one fourth of those taken by them at Shiloh found their graves in rebeldom."[325] By the end of the two days of fighting at Shiloh, the Twelfth Michigan, which had been in the field only ten days prior to the battle, suffered approximately 21 percent losses and 215 combined casualties, with 26 men killed in action; 93 wounded men, many of whom would succumb to their injuries; and 96 men unaccounted for, with the assumption most were prisoners of war.

After the battle, there was considerable confusion both in Company G and among his friends in Lansing as to the welfare and disposition of Captain Cravath. The *Republican* reported it had not heard anything from Cravath since the battle and then reported he was among the wounded arriving at Cincinnati and it was assumed he was sick. In a letter home, Lieutenant Gassimere, who had assumed command of Company G, attempted to update the citizens of Lansing on "where their sons, brothers and neighbors are, and how they are doing.…Capt. Cravath was taken sick with a fever… and went North on board of a steamboat…and has never been heard from."[326] Gassimere stated that they first heard he had died, then that he was, in fact, alive and then heard, again, he had succumbed to the fever. Gassimere ended his letter pleading for any word that could be sent to the company about its captain.

Word finally arrived of the fate of Captain Cravath by way of a Lansing businessman. Joseph E. Warner reported that while with his business associates, including one Dan Rice, in the Toledo railway depot, he noticed six men carrying an invalid soldier onto the cars. Upon inquiring about the soldier's condition, Warner "recognized in the mere skeleton before me, our beloved friend, fellow townsmen and associate, Capt. Cravath…with the brittle thread of life nearly severed.…How great the change, and how terrible the surprise."[327] Cravath recognized his friend from Lansing and, clasping his hand, told him he had nearly entered his eternal home three or four times. Cravath, accompanied by his wife, went to Coldwater, Michigan, to recuperate in the home of his brother-in-law; it was reported that "his escape from the grave [was] almost a miracle."[328] By August, he was well enough to make a short visit to Lansing, although still quite feeble, and by the middle of that month, he returned to command his company. With a resurgence of the symptoms of typhoid fever, however, he was laid low and eventually forced to resign his commission and return to Lansing.

The chance encounter with Lansing businessman Joseph E. Warner bears further description. Warner, although listed as a painter in the 1860 Lansing census, made the majority of his career in the entertainment business. He traveled the Mississippi River as the magician known as "The Wizard of the North." He served as an agent for many circuses, including Spalding and Roger's North American Circus, Forepaugh's Circus and Menagerie and Dan Rice Shows, which was the business that brought him and his employer to Toledo. The Dan Rice Show performed often in Lansing during the war. In the 1870s, Warner formed his own J.E. Warner and Co.'s Great Pacific Circus. The circus had its home in north Lansing on Willow Street with an eighty-acre property (the house still stands) on which numerous animals were wintered, including lions, bears, monkeys and a hippo. Warner served as the thirteenth mayor of Lansing in 1878 and then as a booking agent for the Barnum and Bailey Circus, traveling the world. It was said that Warner was the "most cosmopolitan resident in the city."[329]

On his resignation from Company G, Cravath, after a lengthy convalescence, eventually resumed his duties as editor of the *Lansing State Republican* in April 1863; by August, however, he again, due to faltering health, was not able to work and eventually resigned the position.[330] Cravath spent time in Chicago, seeking the curative properties of "electro thermal baths" at the institute of Dr. Jaye Hayes.[331] He was elected to the Michigan State Senate in 1870, representing Lansing's Twenty-First District, but died of kidney failure during his first term[332]—another casualty of the war, succumbing to illness well after the last shots had been fired.

Elmira Cravath spent several years trying to prove her husband was sickened as a direct result of the typhoid fever he developed from his time spent in camp and on the battlefield at Shiloh. He eventually received a small monthly pension of twenty dollars for the effects of typhoid, contracted in the mud, putrid water and stench of death that was the Battle of Pittsburg Landing. When he died, adding insult to injury, the pension was revoked, and again Elmira was forced to fight for the reinstatement of her claim, her case coming before the U.S. Senate Committee on Pensions in 1875. After

Joseph E. Warner, Lansing businessman, entertainer, circus promoter and postwar mayor of Lansing. *Forest Parke Library and Archives, Capital Area District Library*.

a thorough examination of the records, which included a review of the credentials of several examining Lansing doctors, the twenty-dollar monthly pension was reinstated,[333] an arguably pitiful and insulting renumeration for Elmira's incredible loss.

The lingering effects of the Battle of Shiloh on Company G persisted with the recuperative trip home of Corporal John T. Strong, who was wounded, somewhat ironically, by a large falling tree limb. Strong would eventually return to his regiment with a packet of letters to Company G soldiers from Lansing loved ones.[334] Sergeant Henry Guest was also listed among the fatalities. Guest had been sick for some time; he was endeavoring to return home on a two-month leave when he died aboard the steamer at Pittsburg Landing before it left the dock. The *Republican*, for which he had worked as a printer for four years, stated: "He was a kind, whole-souled, generous hearted young man, and much respected by all who knew him.…He has an aged mother and father…and leaves a wife and child."[335] On September 27, Private Edgar Yawger also died at the Lansing home of his father as a result of disease contracted at Shiloh; he fought in both days of the battle and "served his country with the heroism of a true American soldier."[336] He had been honorably discharged and was sent home to die; he was eighteen years old.

In a bit of good news, it was reported in a letter sent home by John T. Christmas that his life was saved by the efforts of Michigan citizens. Shortly before leaving Niles, the men were given testaments (Bibles). In a skirmish with Confederates in Mississippi, Christmas was shot, but the bullet hit the testament he was carrying in his left breast pocket and took the brunt of the impact, no doubt saving his life: "He was literally clad with the armor of the Gospel."[337] Christmas was in all likelihood underage, only sixteen, when he enlisted, quite possibly using the ruse of many underage enlistees, who wrote the number 18 on a piece of paper, inserted it into a shoe and then, when asked by the recruiting officer, "How old are you?" could honestly state, "I am over 18." It has been estimated approximately 20 percent of Union soldiers were under the age of eighteen. Christmas survived the war and worked as a paper "feeder" at the *Lansing State Republican*. He died in Greenwood, Wisconsin, in 1927, at the ripe old age of eighty-four.

At the end of March 1863, very near the one-year anniversary of the Battle of Shiloh, Lieutenant Gassimere proffered his resignation and was honorably discharged from the service. The *Republican* reported: "Lieut. Gassenmere was with his regiment through the severe sufferings and hardships through which it passed…and was an officer who knew his duty well."[338] Gassimere eventually moved to Chicago with his family and worked again as a house carpenter. Upon his death in 1918, he was brought home to Lansing and buried in Mt. Hope Cemetery.[339]

Although having had their ranks severely depleted at Shiloh, the Twelfth continued to fight, in Tennessee at Metamora and Middleburg, in Mississippi at Mechanicsville and the Siege of Vicksburg and in Arkansas at the Siege of Little Rock, Claredon and Gregory's Landing. On Christmas Eve 1862, while defending a blockhouse at Middleburg, Tennessee, on the Mississippi Central Railroad, a small detachment of the regiment, including men from Lansing's Company G, successfully repulsed numerous attacks by Confederate cavalry under the command of General Earl Van Dorn. Just 115 men of the Twelfth withstood a Confederate force estimated to be 3,000. Prior to the attack, Van Dorn sent an officer under a flag of truce, who rather haughtily demanded the surrender of the outnumbered detachment. Colonel Graves replied: "I have no doubt he [Van Dorn] can whip us, but while he is getting a meal we will try and get a mouthful."[340] After repeated attacks on the blockhouse, the Confederate force abandoned the field, leaving behind 135 killed, wounded and prisoners. The Twelfth lost 6 wounded and 1 killed and had expended over 4,000 rounds of ammunition.

While the Twelfth fought courageously every time they engaged the enemy, the effects of disease continued to plague the regiment; it suffered more deaths from disease "than any other Michigan regiment except the Sixth Michigan Infantry. Of over two thousand Union regiments, the Twelfth Michigan ranked fifteenth in mortality from disease."[341] Among the Lansing men lost to disease was Thomas M. McCurdy, who died in November 1863, while the regiment was stationed at Little Rock, Arkansas. Thomas left behind his eldest brother, James, who had enlisted in the regiment as a private and had risen to the rank of lieutenant by the end of the war. The Company G veterans held Lieutenant McCurdy in such high esteem that a letter of commendation signed by them all was sent to and published by the *Republican*.

Exemplifying the courage and discipline of the men from Lansing were Joseph C. Wardell, age twenty, and his eighteen-year-old younger brother

Battle Flag of the Twelfth Michigan Volunteer Infantry Regiment, designating their Veteran Volunteer status. *Save the Flags.*

John. The Wardell brothers fought together at Shiloh and continued with the regiment almost to the very end. John mustered out at DeVall's Bluff, Arkansas, when his three-year enlistment expired in early 1865,[342] while Joseph reenlisted and achieved the much respected and coveted "Veteran" status—and an even more coveted thirty-day furlough home. While home on furlough, he married Mary Cockran of Delta Township,[343] then rejoined his regiment and was mustered out in early 1866 at Camden, Arkansas.[344] The brothers initially returned to the Lansing area. When Joseph died on March 16, 1931, at the age of ninety, one of the last members of the Twelfth to pass away, several obituaries throughout the state claimed "he had the distinction of having fired the first shot in the Battle of Pittsburg Landing."[345]

The Twelfth Michigan Volunteer Infantry Regiment and the reenlisted men of Company G were mustered out of the service in March 1866, almost a full year after the end of the war. In announcing the regiment's upcoming return to Michigan, the *Lansing State Republican* reported, "Its record is an honorable one, and it fully sustained the honor of the State on every field of duty."[346] The regiment and the men from Lansing had fulfilled the promise made on that snowy February day in Niles four years earlier. They had in fact "done their duty."

Chapter 11

The House of Correction for Juvenile Offenders

The Boys' Reform School at Lansing

One of the first recruits of Captain Cravath's Company G of the Twelfth Michigan Infantry Regiment was a young man named Edward (also known as Edwin) Foster. Foster was eighteen when he enlisted in "The Tigers" on November 16, 1861, at Lansing. It is presumed he saw action with the regiment at the Battle of Shiloh in April 1862, and by September the same year, he was listed as "absent without leave." No further record of his fairly uneventful military life, nor of his civilian life after the war, was preserved. What was unique about Edward was that he enlisted immediately after having been granted an early release from the House of Correction for Juvenile Offenders in Lansing.

In February 1855, the Michigan legislature meeting in Lansing passed "An Act to Establish a House of Correction for Juvenile Offenders."[347] An annual amount of $25,000 was also appropriated to establish and operate the institution. The reform school continued operations under different names for over one hundred years and was eventually closed in 1972. Original oversight of the facility was under a three-member Board of Control, the members having been appointed by the governor with the advice and consent of the Michigan senate. Board terms of office were staggered, so every two years, one position would be open for appointment or reappointment. Permanent positions within the facility were superintendent, assistant superintendent, teacher, steward, matron, physician and chaplain. With the exception of the physician and chaplain, all officers and employees were required to live on-site, in part to guard against escapes from the barred buildings and stockaded compound.

The Boys' Reform School. *Library of Congress, Geography and Map Division.*

The offenders or students—including several girls for the first few years, until coed incarceration was deemed imprudent—who were under the age of sixteen and had been sentenced to prison would instead be sent to the house of correction until they reached the age of twenty-one. The act also established Lansing in the County of Ingham as the site for the institution—provided some suitable piece of land that was at least twenty acres be donated to the state free of all charge.

In 1855, the state was gifted thirty acres of land, and in 1865, it purchased adjoining property, with the site eventually totaling almost two hundred acres. The property was bordered roughly by what is now Michigan, Pennsylvania, Saginaw and Jerome Streets, comprising the approximate area of the grounds of the former Eastern High School and portions of the campuses of Lansing Catholic High School and Sparrow Hospital. The first superintendent was Theodore Foster; assisted by his wife, Frances, he served from the founding of the institution until his resignation in 1860, retaining his membership on the board until shortly before his death in 1865. Foster's successor was the Reverend Danforth Nichols, who served for only one year and was succeeded by Cephas Robinson, who was originally the assistant superintendent; Robinson served until his death in 1866.

In 1857, the institution had 33 boys, but by the fall of 1861, the first year of the war, 145 boys lived or were "incarcerated" at the reform school. Offenders were classified into seven "grades," with all entering offenders automatically going into the lowest grade and then, through merit and study,

Theodore Foster. *Collection of Lille Foster.*

rising to the higher grade. Those "inmates" who broke the policies of the house of correction could be reduced by grades, sentenced to solitary confinement, put on bread and water, deprived of amusements and lastly, when necessary, "corrected" by corporal punishment. The "offenders" would also be "constantly employed in labor during every week, except on the Sabbath."[348] While many of the offenders were outright criminals whose offenses included "whipping a mother" and "burglary," some of the boys were incarcerated for more minor offenses, including "stealing plums." The plum thief "insisted upon being sent to the Reform School, which he had heard of, for said he 'I shall learn a trade there, and have a home, which I never had in my life.'"[349]

While not studying, the boys tended large gardens, which provided crops and vegetables for in-house consumption; in 1862, they produced 519 bushels of potatoes, 175 of oats and 40 of sweet corn; 3 tons of hay, 700 heads of cabbage; and 192 quarts of strawberries.[350] The boys cut wood, providing fuel, and were employed in a number of shops where they contractually manufactured chairs, sewed uniforms for in-house wear, caned chairs and wove palms for hats. This occupied their time, taught them valuable skills and also produced revenue for the institution. For a very brief period during the war, the legislature debated the idea of having the boys produce arms and accoutrements for the war effort. The lack of proper manufacturing equipment and the necessary expenditure of funds to acquire it; the relative isolation of Lansing, which posed supply and shipping problems; and the most obvious imprudence of having incarcerated individuals produce weapons killed the effort.[351] Contributing to this decision was the fact that the main shop at the reformatory had been burned, most likely maliciously, twice during the past two years and had been totally demolished in the most recent fire, which also raised a question: Were these boys misguided youths, desperately needing loving and benevolent direction and reformation, or hardened criminals who required detention and punishment? The answer to both questions appeared to be in the affirmative.

Theodore Foster wrote many letters to his sister Lydia Comstock, who was living in Wisconsin, giving her updates on the progress of the house of correction. He also kept detailed records and provided annual reports to the legislature, as did the superintendents who followed him. These documents shed light upon the reform school, the students/inmates who occupied it and the mindset of the superintendents and the Board of Control, all of which likewise illuminate the reasons for the large army enlistments from the school.

In his early letters, Foster seems to vacillate between running a "Boys Bastille"—as the Democratic papers defined the reform school under his leadership—and a home with a happy but somewhat dysfunctional family.

Frances Delia Seymour Foster. *Collection of Lille Foster.*

> *The boys behave quite well as could be expected, but…many unpleasant things annoy both Frances [Foster's wife] and myself.…Our boys, except two, are all thieves, and our girls are both prostitutes, although the youngest is but eleven years.…The Board tell me that I must consider myself a father to them all. Is not this a hard task? Especially when I am required to make them all into good boys and girls.…The Democrats here publish…the most abominable lies about the government and officers of the Institution. They call us hardhearted, cruel, unfeeling etc.*[352]

In another letter, Foster writes,

> *The Institution has run right along for some time without any jarring.…I have less care and trouble about them than I had at first.…They improve quite as well as could be expected…considering that they are so extremely degraded.…Eight of them go downtown to Church several times a week.…I have doubts how long their goodness will last.*[353]

Foster questions their piety even as he speaks favorably on it. Balancing reform, punishment and recidivism never was and has never been an easy task, and criticism of the superintendents was not always fair or balanced. In 1860, Foster was "eased out of the superintendency,"[354] replaced by Reverend Nichols, and Nichols, too, was in turn soon replaced by Cephas Robinson.

Contributing to the obvious challenges of reform versus punishment were the combined strains of an ever-increasing inmate population and the financial burden this placed upon the institution. "Already by the opening rounds of the Civil War, state and municipal courts had sentenced so many children to the Reform School that the three-member Board of Control and the superintendent had added one wing to their building and were pleading for a capital appropriation to add another....The state barely paid for custodial care and expected the Board…to invent whatever additional resources were needed."[355] In 1861, the school did not receive its full appropriation, due in part to the financial burdens facing the state in prosecuting the war, leaving the reform school with a sizable deficit.

One possible solution to the ever-increasing financial problems was to permit the older boys to enlist under an early release with "conditional tickets of leave,"[356] which could be legally accomplished under recently passed state legislation allowing underage males to enlist with parental or court consent. Encouraging these enlistments might not be onerous, either, given the fact that over fifty recently discharged boys had already enlisted of their own accord.[357] "At the last meeting of the Board of Control, ten of the inmates were deemed worthy of dismissal; and most of these have since joined the military companies organizing in this place."[358] The state and local authorities also started offering bonuses in an attempt to avoid drafting Lansing men to fill the quota under the Conscription Act. Even though records show that many of the bonuses never made it into the hands of the boys and instead went to their errant parents, the money served as a strong inducement to enlist, and many boys were given early release so they could sign up to fight.[359]

Almost half of the Michigan regiments would have at least one—often more than one—reform schoolboy enlisted in its ranks, as would several of the companies formed in Lansing. Of these, 50 enlisted after having served their full sentence, in addition to almost 100 boys granted early release through the "conditional tickets of leave." Records indicate some of the boys were as young as fourteen.[360] By 1863, one-third of the discharged boys, 53 out of the total of 153 discharged since the school commenced, were in the ranks of the Union army.[361] The young men enlisted with the First, Fourth, Seventh and Eighth Michigan Cavalry Regiments and the Second, Fifth, Sixth, Eighth, Twelfth, Fourteenth, Sixteenth, Seventeenth, Eighteenth and Twenty-Seventh through Thirtieth Michigan Infantry Regiments, along with those serving in the First Michigan Engineers and Mechanics, the Michigan Lancers and the First Michigan Light Artillery Regiment. At the conclusion of the war, some of the boys returned to Lansing or reported on their condition through letters to the officers of the school. The *Republican* noted, "The boys who have returned from the army appear well....The fortunes of war have also befallen them. Some have been slain in battle; some have died...some have been wounded...but the greater portion have returned and will commence labor in some useful employment."[362]

Chapter 12

They Covered Themselves in Glory

The First Michigan Volunteer Colored Infantry Regiment/The 102nd United States Colored Troops

S ix reform school enlistees who had been granted early release saw service with the First Michigan Colored Infantry Regiment: George Morgan, Charles Points, Benjamin Brooks, Charles Crockett, Benjamin Green and William Harrison.[363] In addition to the reform schoolboys were three African American men who enlisted in Lansing: Benjamin Cooper, who was a Middle Town barber, Noah Hill and William Howard. When the war began, Black men were not allowed to serve in the Union army, despite many trying repeatedly to enlist. Objections ebbed after the Emancipation Proclamation was issued in 1863 and with the growing realization the Union desperately needed more soldiers. In early 1864, the First Michigan Volunteer Colored Infantry Regiment, composed of Black soldiers and White officers, was mustered into service. Many of the volunteers were escaped slaves who made their way to freedom in Canada through Michigan on the Underground Railroad and returned to the country of their enslavement with the hope of freeing family members still held in bondage in the South. The regiment organized at Camp Ward in Detroit under the leadership of *Detroit Advertiser and Tribune* editor Henry Barnes. Barnes had spent time living in Lansing as the founding editor of the *Lansing State Republican,* the clerk of the Michigan House of Representatives and as a state senator from 1859 to 1860.

On January 5, 1864, the Colored Ladies Aid Society of Detroit presented the regiment with a beautiful flag. The flag, one of several flags carried by the First Michigan Colored Troops during the course of the war, was a regimental with a field of blue emblazoned with the federal eagle with outstretched wings. Beautifully painted upon the banner, at the fore, was the inscription "All men are born free and equal to realize which we fight." The flag was hand-painted by Detroit artist Robert Hopkin of the firm Laible, Wright and Hopkin. Years later, another of the firm's partners, William Wright, executed the nine acres of decorative artwork in the capitol at Lansing.

The First Michigan Colored Troops and the recruits from the reform school suffered many degradations common among Black troops during the war. The regiment was commanded only by white officers. The enlisted men were paid less than white soldiers. Black soldiers earned ten dollars per month with a three-dollar deduction for clothing, while the white privates were paid thirteen dollars per month plus a three-dollar stipend for clothing. In addition, white soldiers, in the last years of the war, earned enlistment bonuses up to several hundred dollars; Black soldiers were initially given none. The Black troops were consistently housed in substandard barracks, often in former pigsties or dwellings open to the elements. Their rations and equipment were woefully lacking, and initially, they were only used for noncombat manual labor—digging trenches, constructing roads and fortifications and destroying Confederate railroads. Black soldiers were also often given no quarter on capture or surrender. By order of the Confederate congress, captured Black soldiers were to be returned to their former masters or turned over to the Confederate state authorities and were subject to the laws of that state, which usually meant execution. Perhaps one of the most painful degradations was the loss of their state regimental designation, as Black regiments were federalized and were not permitted to keep their state designation. The First Michigan Colored Troops was redesignated as the 102nd United States Colored Troops (USCT), making the 102nd the only Michigan regiment to lose its state identity. The men suffered largely in silence.

In 1864, the regiment was finally given an opportunity to fight. The following account was drawn from an unnamed correspondent of the fight of the 102nd at Honey Hill, South Carolina, in December 1864. "On one side of our little detail of 300 men the 54th Massachusetts (colored) was drawn up, on the other side a white regiment, the 127th New York. Here our forces sustained a charge from the enemy and charged in turn. In this affair the 102nd covered themselves in glory. It is acknowledged without stint on all hands that our regiment maintained the steadfast line of battle and fought with the greatest determination of any troops on the ground."[364]

Captain and later Michigan Supreme Court justice Edward Cahill. *Courtesy of the Michigan Supreme Court Historical Society.*

Numerous accounts were given of soldiers being grievously wounded, "shot through and through" and still refusing to leave the line. The regiment would eventually lose almost 10 percent of its strength from disease, wounds and those killed in action.

An important event connecting the regiment to Lansing, state and capitol history was the January 1864 commissioning of Edward Cahill as a white officer with the rank of lieutenant (later captain) in the 102nd USCT. After the war, in 1890, Cahill was appointed by Michigan governor Cyrus Luce as a justice of the Michigan Supreme Court and made Lansing his home. Cahill served on the five member court, three of whom were veterans of the Union army, when in October 1890 it issued its unanimous ruling in *Ferguson v. Gies*. This ruling set the legal precedent in Michigan that separation by race in public places was illegal. The plaintiff, William Webb Ferguson, went on to become Michigan's first African American legislator when he was elected to the Michigan House of Representatives in 1892. There is little doubt Captain and later Justice Cahill recognized the equality of the races when he led these proud, brave Black men, including men from Lansing, into combat.

Tragically, equality for these returning soldiers in the eyes of the law or in the eyes of some Ingham County citizens was not present when in August 1866, John Taylor, who had fought with the 102nd after enlisting in Jackson, was removed by a mob from the Ingham County jail. Taylor was being held for an alleged attack on the family of a local farmer over disputed wages. The mob dragged Taylor out to a tree near the Mason depot and, playing the role of judge and jury, hanged him. "Taylor's lynching is a dark and notable piece of Ingham County's history."[365] Some Lansing men fought and died to uphold the Union; others fought and died for the freedom of others. The sad truth was, real freedom, justice and equality for African Americans, including those living in the Lansing area, was often only a fleeting dream.

Chapter 13

FIRST IN THE REGIMENT

The Fourteenth Michigan Infantry Regiment, Company D, Jeffries Rangers

I n late September 1914, ten elderly, gray-bearded gentlemen gathered in Lansing at the dusty old Grand Army of the Republic hall. They conducted some necessary business, including the election of a slate of officers; shared several meals together; exchanged numerous stories of bygone days; enjoyed some entertainment; and reveled in the bonds of brotherhood forged in battle. They were among the last surviving members of Company D of the Fourteenth Michigan Volunteer Infantry Regiment, and this twentieth reunion would be one of their last.[366]

The Jeffries or Lansing Rangers of Company D formed in the city under the leadership of Captain James J. Jeffries, a thirty-five-year-old Third Ward cabinetmaker turned accomplished homebuilder turned much-respected captain. Jeffries received his commission as captain in October 1861 and immediately commenced recruiting. By February 1862, his company was filled to overflowing with 138 men.[367] "Our company is regarded as one of the first in the regiment."[368]

Among the new recruits of Company D was Cyrus Alsdorf of Lansing. Alsdorf, who was thirty-five and had moved to Lansing in 1856 with his wife, Loretta, was a foreman in the reform school shop. He mustered into the company as a musician, and he was quickly named principal musician of the regiment. Through the course of the war, he would command and serve in three different brigade bands.[369] The band was "composed chiefly of members from Lansing…together with a fifer, drummer and bugler for every company make forty-three musicians, all under the supervision of

Chief Alsdorf."[370] Company D soldiers who served in the regimental band included Francis Holly, Theodore Holmes, William Little, James Dixon and Daniel Mevis.

The Mevis family settled in Lansing in 1847. Daniel's father owned and operated a small hotel on Washington Avenue that was known as the "halfway house," it being halfway between Middle and Lower Town. Daniel served as the first news carrier for the *Republican* and was appointed the first town crier in 1859. He returned to Lansing in December 1862, after having been discharged for disability after a year of service. In 1911, he published his history of the city, titled *Pioneer Recollections, Semi Historic Side Lights on the Early Days of Lansing.* Mevis, or "Uncle Dan," as he was popularly known, was a fixture in Lansing until his death at the Grand Rapids Soldiers Home in 1930 at the age of ninety-two.[371]

Band members, such as Alsdorf, Dixon and Mevis, were principally noncombatants, although Alsdorf was the recipient of a handsome Colt's revolver presented to him by the band members. When not playing, they assisted in removing wounded soldiers from the battlefield, worked with the medical corps and often performed the sad, gruesome but very necessary task of burying the dead. While their important role in boosting morale and inspiring the men to acts of incredible bravery with their martial airs was recognized, as the war progressed and casualties mounted, regimental bands came to be viewed as an unaffordable luxury. Most of them were disbanded in favor of brigade bands only, and even these were greatly reduced by the end of the war.

Joseph Myers also enlisted with Company D as a first sergeant. Sergeant Myers was twenty-three when he enlisted in Lansing and rose through the ranks quickly, becoming a second and first lieutenant, adjutant and then captain. He fought through the entire war and mustered out as acting assistant inspector general of the brigade.

Prior to Company D leaving its regimental camp of instruction in Ypsilanti, on March 8, Captain Jeffries was the recipient of a "magnificent sword." The inscribed sword was presented to him by the noncommissioned officers and privates of Company D. Captain Jeffries, in receiving the gift, proclaimed, "It would never be sheathed until this rebellion was crushed out and peace restored to our land."[372] After an impressive flag-presentation ceremony, attended by Governor Austin Blair, the "Wolverine Fourteenth" left Ypsilanti on April 17 on an enormous thirty-two-car train. Ypsilanti citizens who had comforted and provided aid to the men through their winter training came out "en masse" to say farewell.

Right: Captain Joseph Myers of Lansing. *Archives of Michigan.*

Opposite: Battle flag of the Fourteenth Michigan Volunteer Infantry Regiment. *Save the Flags.*

A corresponding member of Company D, who signed his letters "S.E.R." and was most likely Samuel E. Rogers, reported that after a short stop in Joliet, Illinois, the men were divided into two trains and proceeded to Alton, Illinois, then boarded the steam packet *David Yatum* to St. Louis. From St. Louis, the Fourteenth was ordered to Pittsburg Landing on the Tennessee River, scene of the recent battle. While steaming to the Landing, ships bearing the wounded and dead passed by, and while encamped near Shiloh, the men had the opportunity to visit the battlefield. "The stench of dead horses and burning remains of man and beast, in places is almost unendurable.…The devastation of this beautiful country by the ravages of war, is painful to behold and a reproach to civilization."[373] The Fourteenth then participated in the siege of Corinth, Mississippi, and in November had a sharp battle at Lavergne, Tennessee. In January 1863, they engaged the enemy again at the Battle of Stones River. Later that year, the regiment was

temporarily mounted, and it spent the majority of 1863 pursuing guerilla bands around Franklin, Brentwood and Nashville, Tennessee.

In January 1864, the men veteranized with 414 reenlisting; this was done with the promise they could remain mounted troops. The men came home to Michigan for their thirty-day veteran furlough and, upon returning to Nashville, received word they would be returned to infantry duty and would not be mounted. Despite their protests, they eventually submitted to the inevitable, were attached to General Sherman's army and took part in the Atlanta Campaign, the Battles of Kennesaw Mountain and Chattahoochee River and the Siege of Atlanta and Jonesboro. On July 10, Captain Jeffries succumbed to disease in Chattanooga, brought on by exposure in the field, and was buried in the national cemetery there, sheathing his sword one last time. In a resolution offered by Company D, the author stated, "We deeply regret his death....No words can portray the honor and respect we entertain for one who so long and so faithfully sustained the cause of Union and Liberty."[374]

That fall, Company D marched with Sherman's army to the sea and Savannah, Georgia, and then, in early 1865, through South and North Carolina—while constantly skirmishing with the enemy. The regiment had its final severe battle from March 19 to 21 at Bentonville, North Carolina, while counterattacking a Confederate force, resulting in hand-to-hand combat. At the close of the war, they were marched to Goldsboro, then to Raleigh and on to Richmond and Washington, D.C., where they marched in the triumphant Grand Review parade. From D.C., the men were sent to Louisville, Kentucky, where they were mustered out, paid off and disbanded on July 29, 1865.[375]

Cyrus Alsdorf was one of the few men who survived and came home to Lansing. He resumed his old job at the reform school and later owned and operated a drugstore with his son, becoming "one of the most prosperous businessmen in the city."[376] James Dixon also survived and worked as a tailor in postwar Lansing until his death in 1874. Of the estimated 150 men who saw action with Company D, only 50 returned, with 100 lost to disease, killed in battle, captured or reported as missing in action.

Chapter 14

Nothing Can Beat
the Michigan Soldiers

Sixteenth Michigan Volunteer Infantry Regiment, Company G

T he Sixteenth Michigan Infantry, originally known as Stockton's Independent Regiment, recruited throughout Michigan, and Lansing men served in several companies, principally in Company G under the command of First Lieutenant Jacob Weber. Before the war, the German-born brewer and father of three[377] was the commander of the Williams German Light Artillery, a counterpoint to the Williams Rifles, both named after Adolphus Williams. The Williams or German Light Artillery was a state-recognized and partially state-funded militia group that in 1860 received a one-hundred-dollar appropriation from the state military fund; it had twenty-one active members, one brass cannon and twenty musketoons.[378] Weber and Lieutenant George Gassimere, who later served as first lieutenant in Company G of the Twelfth Michigan Infantry, commanded the unit, and many of the men enlisted with Weber as infantry in the Sixteenth Regiment.

The morning of August 19, 1861, the company left Lansing, witnessed by a large number of citizens, the mayor, the Common Council, city firemen and the band. They were escorted as far as Lower Town, where Captain Weber delivered parting words and "pledged himself not to disgrace the land of his adoption."[379] To the tune of "Hail Columbia," they were loaded onto wagons volunteered by citizens, transported to cars and delivered to their rendezvous at Camp Blair, Detroit.

Alexander Cameron, born in County Down, Ireland, was thirty, the father of three and working as a Second Ward clerk before enlisting.[380] He sent many reports of Company G and the Sixteenth Infantry to the *Republican*. In one of his first letters, in January 1862, written from Hall's Hill, Virginia, he reported on the condition of the Lansing boys: "Let our friends at home not be alarmed about our comfort as to food or clothing.... We are well fed, well clothed....The men have every confidence in the staff and line officers."[381] By April, the regiment, along with many other Michigan regiments, was encamped on the peninsula and engaging the enemy, with Cameron reporting that no less than six Michigan regiments "were within stones-throw of each other....The Lansing boys have a good time for a day or so visiting each other....Judging from the positions that the Michigan regiments occupy, they are highly esteemed...though not blinded to the almost certainty of large sacrifice of life...leaving hundreds to mourn an irreplaceable loss."[382]

Alexander Cameron was born in Ireland and settled in Lansing, working as a clerk before his enlistment in the Sixteenth Regiment. *Collection of Scott Shattuck.*

By June, "the irreplaceable" losses became all too real. At the Battle of Gaines' Mill on the peninsula on June 27, the Sixteenth fought off numerous Confederate charges: "Six times they attacked...and were repulsed with fearful slaughter....They dashed down upon us like a torrent...leaving the field literally strewn with the dead."[383] In Cameron's account, Union general Butterfield complimented the regiment, stating, "Nothing can beat the Michigan soldiers."[384] "Our artillery opened upon them, mowing them down like grain before the reaper....Company G lost one-third of what it took into the field, with the regimental losses estimated at 150 men."[385] Among the Lansing men killed was nineteen-year-old James Vanarsdall and John S. Gardner. Gardner was twenty, and before enlisting, he was a Third Ward laborer living with his mother and saddle-and-harness-maker father; he also left behind two younger brothers.[386] Alexander Cameron was also wounded but survived and was promoted to first sergeant. The Battles of Malvern Hill, Second Bull Run and Fredericksburg followed.

Orderly Sergeant Cameron was sent home to Lansing that fall to recruit, with his office over Bertch's meat market on Washington Avenue. Cameron enticed recruits with advertisements in the paper. "Evade the draft and thereby secure the large bounties offered....Between citizens and

Battle flag of the Sixteenth Michigan Volunteer Infantry Regiment. *Save the Flags.*

Government bounties the amount is $188.00….By volunteering you are able to say who shall officer you…kind and true officers….Company G, was raised in this city by Capt. Weber….Braver and kinder officers cannot possibly exist."[387]

In January, Captain Weber resigned, and Cameron was commissioned second lieutenant on April 17, 1863. Three months later, on July 2, while commanding Company G, he lost his right arm and was severely wounded in the right side in the bloody fight defending Little Round Top on the extreme left flank of the Union army at Gettysburg. His service, however, was not over. After being commissioned a captain, he was appointed chief of the Ambulance Department of the South, and at the end of the war, he returned to Lansing, one of many who would display the unenviable soldier's badge of courage.

With the construction of the new capitol in 1879, the state continued a longstanding tradition of offering employment opportunities to returning veterans, especially those who had been permanently disabled by the loss of limbs. This tradition was continued in modern times and through the latter wars, with many veterans finding suitable and honorable employment within the walls of the capitol. Alexander Cameron was likewise employed as a clerk in the swamp land commissioner's office and later as a night watchman.[388]

In December 1863, 294 members of the Sixteenth having reenlisted, they were sent home on veteran's furlough, and upon returning to Virginia, the litany of battles continued: the Wilderness, Spotsylvania, North Anna, Bethesda Church, Cold Harbor, Petersburg. In the fall of 1864, election officials were sent to the front to collect the Michigan soldiers' votes. In a letter to the *Republican*, an unidentified member of the Sixteenth wrote, "I am now old enough to be a voter, and I shall vote for the Union every time"[389]—this despite the unending casualties suffered by his regiment at Dabney's Mills, Hatcher's Run, White Oak Swamp, Quaker Road and Five Forks, Virginia, all leading to Lee's eventual surrender. On July 25, 1865, the remnants of the Sixteenth Infantry, including the few surviving members of Company G, arrived at Jackson, Michigan. There, they were paid off and disbanded. Their battle flag served as a testament to the hard service they performed, with its long list of painted battle honors.

Chapter 15

WE HAVE GIVEN OF THE BEST WE HAVE

The Twentieth Michigan Volunteer Infantry Regiment, Company A

The summer of 1862 brought ever-increasing casualties, and with the war going badly for the Union, President Lincoln issued a call for 300,000 additional troops. To meet Michigan's quota of 11,686 men, the cull was divided among the state's six congressional districts. Each district supplied one infantry regiment, with an additional regiment, the Twenty-Fourth, from Wayne County. The balance was made with cavalry and artillery units forming at large and new recruits attributed to the regiments already engaged. Seventeen infantry regiments were already in the field, so the newly formed regiments were numbered eighteen to twenty-four. Under these conditions, the Twentieth Michigan Volunteer Infantry Regiment formed in Michigan's Third Congressional District, which included Ingham County and Lansing.[390]

Company A, "the first company" of the Twentieth, formed in Lansing, and many of the recruits were the owners of businesses, their sons or state department employees working in the capital city. The company was placed under the leadership of fellow state employee William Huntington Smith. Smith was working in Lansing as the deputy auditor general and was commissioned as second lieutenant and recruiting officer of Company A. The first lieutenant was Darius Calkins of Lansing, who served with Company B, Second U.S. Sharpshooters, but had resigned due to failing health and on regaining his strength accepted this new commission.

The colonel of the Twentieth, Adolphus Wesley Williams, moved to Lansing from New York and was living with his wife, Polly, and children in

Captain William Huntington Smith was a deputy auditor for the state, working in Lansing, before the war. *Archives of Michigan.*

the Second Ward.[391] Williams, a veteran of the Mexican-American War, owned a jewelry store and organized a prewar Lansing militia company, the Williams Rifles, and the smaller Williams Light Artillery. When the war began, he accepted a commission as major in the Second Michigan. He saw action at the Battle of Bull Run on July 21, 1861, where "he was left in command of the Second… and acquitted himself with honor."[392] In March 1862, Williams was commissioned as lieutenant colonel and was three times wounded at Yorktown, Williamsburg and Fair Oaks, Virginia, during the Peninsula Campaign.[393] Although honorably discharged for disability and suffering from typhoid fever,[394] in the summer of 1862, he accepted the commission as colonel of the Twentieth.

Recruiting for these new regiments proved challenging, as the state had already sent tens of thousands of volunteers to the field, although the specter of an upcoming draft loomed large and served as an enlistment incentive. The August 4, 1862 War Department Draft Proclamation stated that by August 15, a mandatory draft would be implemented in states not meeting their quota. Two days later, the *State Republican* reported forty men had enlisted in Company A, this "notwithstanding the fact that we are in the midst of the harvest."[395] Attempting to avoid the last resort of drafting men, localities offered bonuses, and Lansing donations guaranteed every man who enlisted with Company A a twenty-dollar bonus.

It is unclear whether the bonus, patriotism or the impending draft led to the fact that one week later, Smith's company was filled beyond capacity with 121 recruits.[396] On Friday, August 14, the evening before its departure to join the regiment in Jackson, the company partook of a special dinner in Representative Hall and then "repaired to the senate chamber and enjoyed themselves in the mazes of dance."[397] Upon arriving in Jackson the following afternoon, the novice recruits awkwardly set up their tents on the regimental campground one mile from the heart of the city. "We do not think that a company has been raised in the State that embraces more real merit and intelligence.…They are the cream of our county.…No man with a heart in his breast can look upon this fine body of young men, going forth to battle…without having feelings well up within him.…May God bless them and watch over them.…We have given of the best we have."[398]

Among Company A's noncommissioned officers were Second Sergeant William M. Greene, Third and Fourth Corporals Albert E. Cowles and Henry V. Hinckley and Sixth Corporal Harmon Paddleford. Greene was twenty and living with his parents while reading the law. Cowles was a twenty-two-year-old graduate of the first class at the Michigan Agricultural College and the son of one of Lansing's founding fathers, Joseph P. Cowles. Hinckley was thirty-two and the owner of Lansing's only tobacco and cigar shop, two doors down from Thayer's Drugstore in Middle Town. "Our friend Hinckley is now in the ranks…but his tobacco and cigar store still runs."[399] Paddleford was a twenty-five-year-old painter from the Third Ward.[400]

Since leaving home at the age of thirteen, Henry Brooks Baker had attended school intermittently, supporting himself by teaching and working other odd jobs; by 1860, he was clerking at a Lansing hotel.[401] He attended lectures in medicine and chemistry at the University of Michigan and read medicine with Lansing doctor Ira Hawley Bartholomew,[402] who served as the mayor of Lansing the last two years of the war. On August 18, 1862, Baker mustered into Company A as a twenty-four-year-old private; the next day, he was promoted to hospital steward. After service at the Battle of Fredericksburg in December 1862 as an operating table assistant, he was promoted to assistant surgeon and was the assistant surgeon in charge of three hospital wards. Baker would serve the medical needs of his men at the company, regimental, brigade, division and corps levels through the entire war. After the war, he received his formal medical degree and provided care to the citizens of Lansing in practice with his mentor, Dr. Bartholomew. In 1873, Dr. Baker became the first secretary and founder of the Michigan State Board of Health. His strong belief that an "organized approach to sanitation could reduce death"[403] was no doubt the result of his war experience.

Another early Lansing medical recruit was Orville Pattison Chubb. The thirty-one-year-old was a graduate of Wesleyan-Michigan Union College in Leoni Township near Jackson, a school known for its strong abolitionist views and one of the first coed institutions in the nation.[404] Chubb then attended the Cincinnati Medical College in Ohio.[405] Some sources have Chubb practicing medicine, while another lists him as working in a "lucrative position in the State House at Lansing."[406] Irrespective of his position, Chubb enlisted as a private, and he, too, was soon promoted to acting assistant surgeon, then assistant surgeon; he would muster out at the war's end as

Left: Dr. Henry Brooks Baker of Lansing enlisted as a private but soon rose through the ranks of the army medical corps despite his lack of a medical degree. He received his degree after the war and founded the Michigan State Board of Health. *From* Portrait and Biographical Album of Ingham and Livingston Counties, Michigan.

Right: Dr. Orville Pattison Chubb enlisted as a private in Company A of the Twentieth Michigan Infantry and cared for the men through their entire service, including the trench warfare of Petersburg, Virginia. *Archives of Michigan.*

brigade surgeon.[407] Chubb, who understandably became disenchanted with medicine as a result of his horrendous wartime experiences, moved in 1866 to Fairmont, Minnesota, where he became a pillar of the community and engaged in peaceful pursuits, including bridge building, farming and brickmaking.[408]

As custom dictated, many of the men were the recipients of sashes, swords and other accouterments before their departure for Jackson. Lansing Orderly Sergeant Benjamin Berry received a beautiful silk sash as a sign of the "love and respect the boys have already manifested for him."[409] Captain Smith likewise received a draft of fifty-five dollars for the purchase of a sword from his fellow friends, the officers and clerks of the state departments. In presenting the draft, his colleague in the auditor general's office, Ezra Jones,[410] stated, "You sir, nor the brave and intelligent men you command, have no love of war, no thirst for blood, no unhallowed revenge burning in your hearts....You have heard and heeded your country's call....We are sure that if you fall you will fall with your face to the foe."[411] Captain Smith responded, "Officers of the State Departments and Brother Clerks: I accept the memento as a token of friendship.…I feel that I have yet to earn the ownership to so valuable a gift. When that is done, and not till then, shall I say in good faith, 'Tis mine.'… Brothers, I thank you, and bid you all good-bye."[412]

Corporal Cowles became a faithful correspondent to his friends and family through the columns of the *Republican*. In a letter dated September 7, he reported that the men waited in the rain in Jackson for the late arrival of the train. The train proceeded to Detroit, carrying its cold, drenched passenger-soldiers, passing through Grass Lake, Chelsea, Ann Arbor and Ypsilanti, with the citizens at each stop supplying baskets of fruit, pies and cakes. Upon arriving in Detroit, they marched to the ferryboat dock of *The Morning Star* and *The May Queen*. Finding the steerage compartment "barely fit for hogs," the men took spots topside wherever limited space was available. On arriving in Cleveland after their nighttime, "rather rough" passage on Lake Erie, they again boarded cars for Pennsylvania. Each town greeted the train with waving handkerchiefs, flags and smiles from the ladies. Corporal Hinckley secured the address of one of the prettiest of the young ladies, but Cowles reported, "I can't imagine what he intends to do with it, unless he means to forward her a quantity of cigars and tobacco."[413] In Pittsburgh, the citizens prepared a full supper for the entire one-thousand-man regiment: "They have a meal ready for every regiment that passes through."[414] Some of the boys proclaimed they would settle in Pittsburgh after the war, due to the kind treatment they received there. Through a fortunate mix-up, the sleeping car reserved for the regimental officers was instead occupied by the privates and officers of Company A, traveling to Baltimore in a fashion they found "very acceptable."[415] They then proceeded to Washington and marched about two miles south through Alexandria to Fort Lyon, just outside the city.

While encamped near D.C., many of the soldiers toured the city, "gazing at the Presidential mansion, Treasury, Patent and Post Office buildings and admiring the magnificent proportions and splendid architecture of the Capitol." Corporal Henry Carpenter said "he had lived more within the last week than in all his previous life."[416] The men were fortunate in having their friend and former tobacco salesman Hinckley along: "He keeps the boys in good humor by generously dispensing among them the 'necessary weed.'" Sadly, army fare did not compare to Lansing and "the well-furnished tables at the Benton House or Eagle."[417] Attempting to keep the men provisioned and adequately fed was a challenge. "It seemed tough to the boys to be put upon the march without anything to eat"[418]—this despite the efforts of former Lansing resident John Hartwell Treadwell. Treadwell, known as "Hart," was with the regiment as a civilian sutler, keeping them supplied with the comforts of home, at a price.

In October, Captain Smith was promoted to major. Cowles reported he was a gentleman, a kind-hearted man and a good officer, and the men were glad to see him promoted. Lieutenant Calkins was likewise promoted to captain, although the lingering effects of fever eventually necessitated his resignation. Cowles reported Henry Baker was doing well in his role as hospital steward and Dr. Chubb "is endowed with a heart and is in a place where its goodness can be felt and appreciated."[419] The regiment was soon marching an average fifteen miles a day toward Sharpsburg, Maryland, near the site of the recent bloody battle. Colonel Williams "is very careful of his men and is becoming very popular among them." Despite this consideration, Cowles also stated, "The soldier seldom knows where he is going.…Like a horse, he is harnessed into his trappings and driven along till he is stopped. He is well broke and moves along very docile…until he falls in his tracks from exhaustion."[420] The regiment witnessed the effects of battle: devastated farms, shell-marked buildings and churches and homes filled to capacity with the wounded and the dying, including the home where their Lansing friend Lieutenant Jack Whitman died. They encountered other friends from Lansing who had fought in the battle, some of them grievously wounded. "Since we have been here, we have exchanged visits with the boys of the old regiments, and I believe we have now seen all the boys from Lansing."[421] They also participated in a grand review of the troops by Generals McClellan and Burnside and President Lincoln.

By November, the men were again on the march, this time into Virginia, through the seat of secession and "making traitors hunt their holes."[422] Although outright theft of property was discouraged with varying degrees of success and was often dependent on the commanding officer's consideration, armies most often were forced to live off the land. Cowles reported firewood was essential: "Wood must be had, and fences must fall.…Chickens and turkeys must roost high not to be found by the soldier. The boys also appear to have a hankering after fresh pork and mutton."[423] In one comical case of foraging, Wilber Dubois, whose experience on his family farm in Lansing should have served him better, encountered an angry bee after stealing some comb from a rebel hive and biting down on one of its surly Confederate inhabitants, the welt "causing a slight momentary addition to his former beauty."[424] Dubois survived "his wounding" and by 1864 had risen in rank and was a second lieutenant of the 108th United States Colored Infantry.[425]

Corporal Harmon Paddleford died in November 1862. He was one of many Lansing men who succumbed to disease. *Archives of Michigan.*

Company A continued to lose men along the march as a result of sickness. Orderly Sergeant William Green, in command of the company, reported Lieutenant Calkins was left in hospital, as were Sergeants Haviland, Carpenter, Hudson and Paddleford, the ranks being reduced to only fifty-six men.[426] Corporal Paddleford died in hospital in Maryland on November 30, one of the first Lansing casualties of the company, leaving behind his widowed mother and two younger siblings. He was a volunteer fireman with the Torrent Engine Company No. 1[427] and was "a fine young man, a good soldier, greatly esteemed....His loss is sincerely lamented."[428]

On December 14, Private Andrew Morehouse also succumbed to disease. The Morehouse family were Third Ward shoemakers; Andrew and his older brothers Thomas and Stephen had all enlisted on the same day with Company A. The bodies of Paddleford and Morehouse were embalmed and shipped to Lansing, and both boys were buried on December 29, from the Lansing Episcopal and Methodist Churches, with full Masonic orders at the grave. Many of the Company A boys had been made Master Masons just a few days before their departure.[429] Mrs. Paddleford offered "her sincere thanks to the Masons, and other friends in Lansing, for their aid and sympathy to her, in her recent sad affliction."[430]

Modern arterial embalming was in its infancy during the war and was perfected and championed by New Yorker Dr. Thomas Holmes, whose secret formula made possible the long-term preservation of bodies. While serving in the Union medical corps, he used new techniques to preserve the bodies of soldiers for shipment home. The original cost was one hundred dollars, and it was reported Dr. Holmes alone embalmed over four thousand officers and men.[431] Dr. Holmes's services were advertised throughout the North, including in the Lansing paper.[432] He purportedly left instructions that when he died, his body should *not* be embalmed.

The day Private Morehouse died, his brothers were at the Battle of Fredericksburg, Virginia. Although the Twentieth was not actively engaged and its role "was that of a connecting link, and a reserve," the ill effects of the terrible Union slaughter were keenly felt[433]—so much so that in a letter dated January 24, 1863, in the midst of the ill-fated "mud march," Colonel Williams, who was clearly disheartened, bemoaned the fact that officers were appointed through connections and not based on merit: "The commissions rest upon no ability but that of raising a certain number of noses and toes…a number of useless and discreditable officers and physically disabled men and boys, who fill our hospitals, and finally, graves.[434]

In March, Lieutenant Colonel Smith came home for a short visit and returned to the regiment, which had been shipped to Kentucky, with letters from loved ones and a box of "Segars" (cigars) from the Benton House. Henry Hinckley transferred to the newly formed First Michigan Sharpshooters Regiment as a first lieutenant. In this same month, Albert Hudson, age twenty-one, died of disease, also leaving his widowed mother to grieve his premature passing. Hudson's death was long and painful; in his six months in the hospital, he had been afflicted with diarrhea, typhoid fever and, finally, diphtheria.[435] His oldest brother, Edwin, enlisted with him as a noncommissioned officer and would rise through the ranks to first lieutenant, ending the war as Company A's commanding officer.[436]

Colonel Williams had not been well during the late winter and spring campaigns of 1863, and in his absence, command had reverted to Lieutenant Colonel Smith, as was the case in early May. While home on leave, Williams had regained enough strength to return to his command when he and his wife were in a carriage accident. Williams suffered a broken collarbone and three broken ribs.[437] Williams eventually resigned his commission due to his failing health and was honorably discharged in 1863, with the brevet rank of brigadier general for "gallant and meritorious service."[438] He returned to Lansing, where he served as a Second Ward alderman. In 1875, Williams, along with Lansing dentist Jacob Lanterman and their families, moved to California. They purchased 5,745 acres north of Los Angeles, in La Canada,[439] hoping to establish a community for Michiganders and a health resort.[440] Williams battled the effects of his war injuries, the carriage accident and sickness, including tuberculosis, and died on March 11, 1879.[441]

Shortly after Williams's departure, on Sunday morning, May 10, 1863, the regiment and Company A had their first taste of real combat on the banks of the Cumberland River at Horseshoe Bend, Kentucky. The 250 men, plus a small force of dismounted cavalry, were attacked by Confederate general John Hunt Morgan, with a force eight times their number. The Twentieth sustained 26 casualties, including 3 men killed. Among the dead was Lieutenant Greene of Lansing.[442] Greene was shot in the back during a retreat in an open field, while "leading his men most gallantly."[443] Early in the battle, he had cast aside his sword and picked up a repeating rifle, in order to add firepower to his small detachment. After his wounding, Lansing men H.B. Carpenter and Wilber Dubois dragged their friend to a creek bed, but amid the rebel onslaught and after Greene had died, they were unable to retrieve his personal effects or his body. "Another of the brave sons that our city has sent forth to lay down their lives for their country…young Greene was among the first to fall.…He was beloved by his men and full of promise for the future. What hopes fell with him."[444] In a sad twist of fate, in the same newspaper edition reporting Lieutenant Greene's death was published his last letter home to his father, dated May 4, just six days before the battle that ended his young life. After receiving word of Greene's death, Theodore Foster wrote, "This morning, Miss Pratt, one of our neighbors, who lost a brother in S. Carolina, in the Mich. 8th, called on my daughter, who lost a brother in Virginia, in the Mich. 3d., to go with her and console with Miss Green, whose only brother has just been killed."[445]

In June 1863, Albert Cowles was discharged "when he was brought to Lansing to die";[446] fortunately, he recovered his health, and the next spring, he married Fannie Foster. Cowles served as city attorney and city clerk, probate judge and as a proud member of the Charles T. Foster Post of the Grand Army of the Republic, which had been named after his lamented brother-in-law. Fannie died in 1889, and while visiting Los Angeles in 1906, Albert was struck and killed by a streetcar.[447]

The summer of 1863 found the Twentieth engaged near Vicksburg and then near the capital city of Jackson, Mississippi. After the fall of Vicksburg, the regiment was sent to Kentucky, where it spent most of the summer before taking to the roads to east Tennessee. On November 16, near the small crossroads town of Campbells Station, Tennessee, on a stream named Turkey Creek, the Second, Seventeenth and Twentieth Michigan Infantry regiments engaged the enemy in a severe fight. In the battle, the Twentieth "suffered its greatest loss in the death of Lieutenant Colonel W. Huntington Smith, who fell, pierced through

Albert E. Cowles

Corporal Albert E. Cowles of Lansing saw action with the Twentieth from its organization until his discharge for severe illness in May 1863. *From* Past and Present of the City of Lansing and Ingham County, Michigan.

the brain with a rebel bullet.…Colonel Smith was in every respect a model soldier.…His excellent example inspired cheerfulness under hardship and resolute devotion to duty."[448] Lieutenant Colonel Smith had truly earned the sword presented to him in Lansing only one year earlier: "Tis Mine brothers, I bid you all good-bye."[449]

The year 1864 brought almost continuous action for the Twentieth as a part of General Grant's Overland Campaign through Virginia, terminating in the trenches outside Petersburg. The letters from Dr. Chubb were filled with the growing casualty lists of the Company A boys, which citizens felt compelled to read but did so with the dreaded fear of finding the names of loved ones. Former Lansing clerk Corporal Horace Turner was killed in action near Fredericksburg; forty-three-year-old Corporal William Raynor died of wounds received at the Wilderness, leaving behind his wife, Lydia, now twice widowed, and five children; Lieutenant Henry Carpenter was severely wounded at Cold Harbor, as was Adjutant Benjamin Berry, who was discharged as a result of his wounds. Corporal Ranselas Burlingame was wounded in action and discharged. Dr. Chubb's sad duty did not go unnoticed: "No man has been more unremitting in attention to the wounded.…He has been with them, and under the most galling fire he has received the fallen brave with his own hands."[450]

On June 29, a condolence letter appeared in the columns of the *Lansing State Republican* written by William A. Dewey of Leslie, who was commissioned captain of Company A the previous December. "Mrs. C.W. Coryell: Dear Madam—It becomes my painful duty to inform you that no tidings of a cheering nature concerning the fate of your husband, at the battle of Spottsylvania Court House, that occurred on the 12th day of May last, has been received."[451] Cyrus Coryell was a painter and was well known throughout the community. "He has nobly shared every danger through which we have been called to pass.…He signalized himself by his bravery and manly bearing.…You have to mourn the loss of a brave man and warm-hearted companion."[452] Ironically, this letter was published eleven days after Captain Dewey himself was killed in action near Petersburg, Virginia, along with Private Thomas Cronk and, later that fall, Adjutant Jacob E. Siebert of Lansing. Dr. Chubb bemoaned the situation in the trenches of Petersburg, noting almost every wounding was fatal due to "the head and upper portions of the body being the parts mainly exposed."[453]

In the early morning of July 30, 1864, the Union army exploded a mined tunnel under the Confederate works at Petersburg, creating a huge crater. On the eve of battle, Colonel Byron Cutcheon wrote that for the men of the

Left: Cyrus W. Coryell died on May 19, 1864, from wounds received at the Battle of Spotsylvania, Virginia. *Archives of Michigan.*

Right: Captain William A. Dewey of Leslie entered service with Company A as a second lieutenant and was commissioned captain of Company A. He was killed in action outside of Petersburg, Virginia, on June 18, 1864. *Archives of Michigan.*

Twentieth, the full realization that on the morrow they were to "charge upon a fortified position, under a storm of shot, shell, canister, and bullets, did not add at all to the soundness of our slumbers."[454] Cutcheon stated he did not sleep that night, gazing at the stars and wondering if he should ever see them again. The men then moved silently to the works.[455] The Battle of the Crater brought with it accompanying casualties. Jerome Kroll and John Hailstone were captured and spent the rest of the war in Confederate prisons,[456] their Lansing families unsure of their fate. Prior to the war, Hailstone worked in a Lansing blacksmith shop making fanning mills, which were used to separate grain from chaff, perhaps the most fitting analogy to the effects of war on soldiers and their families.

After the failed Battle of the Crater, the soldiers again settled into trench warfare. By February 1865, only two of the original officers remained, and

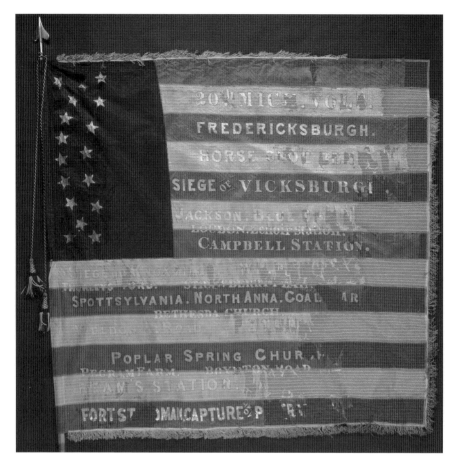

Battle flag of the Twentieth Michigan Infantry. *Save the Flags.*

the regiment was reduced to 150 men fit for duty, out of the 1,000 who left Jackson in the fall of 1862—and the casualties continued. On February 10, Augustus Stevens, who was a farmer from Lansing, was killed in the trenches of Petersburg while carrying provisions to the men.[457] On April 17, one week after General Robert E. Lee's surrender, Elisha Mosher died in Lansing from the emaciation and disease he suffered in the Confederate prisons where he had spent the last six months, one of the last casualties of the once strong and proud company. Mosher was a farmer and had enlisted in Company A with his two brothers, Albert and William, who survived him.[458]

On Saturday, June 10, 1865, the remnants of Company A returned to Lansing to a well-deserved hero's welcome and a special dinner at the

American House Hotel. In his farewell order no. 101 to the men of the Twentieth, General Orlando B. Willcox, a fellow Michigander, wished that the men who remained would "long live to enjoy the reward of well doing and lofty patriotism in the happiness of honorable homes and the admiration of their countrymen."[459]

Chapter 16

To Live Honored and Die Regretted

First Michigan Sharpshooters, Company E

Asahel W. Nichols was born in 1838, the son of a Canadian farmer who had immigrated and settled in Ionia County, Michigan. As a young man, Asa moved to Lansing, and in 1860, he was living with and working as an apprentice to Benjamin Buck in his carpentry and furniture shop.[460] On December 2, 1860, Asa married Sarah Hinckley,[461] the sister of Lansing tobacconist Henry Hinckley. Nichols was secretary of Lansing's Hook and Ladder Company No. 1 and of the Lansing Masonic Lodge No. 33 and served on the executive committee of the Lincoln Wide Awake Club.[462] In 1862, at age twenty-four, he enlisted as the captain of Company E of the First Michigan Sharpshooters Regiment.

While several companies of sharpshooters had already formed in Michigan, including two from Lansing, they were attached to federal regiments consisting of men from many states; this regiment was unique in that the entire body were Michiganders and they retained their state regimental designation. Company K of the regiment, well over one hundred men, was composed of members of the Anishinaabe First Nations peoples of northern Michigan. In October, Nichols began recruiting for his company, concentrating his efforts in Jackson and Lansing.[463] Twelve men from Lansing eventually enlisted with the regiment, and in May 1863 Henry Hinckley, Asahel's brother-in-law, became second lieutenant after his transfer from the Twentieth Michigan.[464]

Among the later recruits joining Company E was Mark Child. Child was a compositor at the *Republican* and, at fifty, was one of the oldest enlisted men.

He attempted to enlist several times but was refused entry on account of his advanced age; undeterred, he was finally admitted to the Sharpshooters. "All honor to his gray hairs. May his life be spared to see our beloved country again united and happy....A noble example is his, and worthy of imitation."[465] At the other extreme in age was Eli Nichols (no known relation to Asa), age fourteen, who enlisted with Company I in Jackson but lived in Lansing. Eli was the eldest of six children; his father was a First Ward cooper. Eli would earn promotion and end the war as a corporal.

Organization of the regiment commenced originally at Kalamazoo, with final completion taking place at Dearborn, where six companies were mustered. In July 1863, the six companies were sent to Indiana to repel the Confederate raider John Hunt Morgan, where they had several skirmishes with the enemy. After their return to Dearborn, an additional four companies enlisted, and in August, the regiment was sent to Chicago to Camp Douglas to guard Confederate prisoners.[466] That fall, newly promoted Sergeant Joseph Kilbourn was sent home to Lansing on recruiting duty, with the promise to new recruits of $150 bonuses. Kilbourn's family were farmers, and prior to enlisting, Joseph was a student at the State Agricultural College in East Lansing. In November, Captain Nichols also returned for a short visit with his wife.[467] A sharpshooter correspondent to the *Republican* reported in January that the boys were doing fine, well fed and sheltered but that constant guard duty was trying, especially when the men were concerned about the well-being of their families in Lansing. A further report in February stated that the men "were burning with impatience to take the field."[468]

By the spring of 1864, the Sharpshooters were attached to the Army of the Potomac and were almost constantly engaged in the battles of the Overland Campaign, including the Wilderness, Spotsylvania, North Anna, Bethesda Church, Cold Harbor and Petersburg. On April 28, compositor Mark Child's life was not spared, as he died from the effects of disease contracted in the field. On June 19, Lieutenant Hinckley wrote to the *Republican* from the trenches outside of Petersburg: "I am alive and well, after participating for three days in one of the most desperate battles of the War....My regiment are nearly all taken prisoners, we only number 62 men....They were on one side of the breast works and our Regiment on the other only four feet apart....Our boys put the muzzle of their guns in the faces of the enemy and fired."[469] Hinckley went on to report that shortly after taking numerous Confederate prisoners, the Sharpshooters were outflanked and most were forced to surrender or be killed. Among those taken prisoner was James Sharkey of Lansing, an Irish-born day laborer from the First Ward. Hinckley, however, had taken a Confederate officer as prisoner and was able to run the gauntlet to the safety of the Union lines, using the officer as a shield.

That summer, Captain Nichols returned to Lansing, after having been confined in hospital in D.C. from the effects of severe sunstroke at Cold Harbor. His return to Michigan was in anticipation of his receiving an officer's commission in the recently formed Twenty-Ninth Michigan Infantry. The appointment, however, never materialized, and in October, he was sent back to his command, then stationed at Weldon Railroad, outside of Petersburg, Virginia. That fall, Colonel Charles Deland was wounded and taken prisoner, and with his appointment as major on December 3, Nichols took over command of the Sharpshooters.[470] The regiment continued service in the trenches of Petersburg in the early months of 1865, and in February it was reported that it was "in fine condition and under the command of Major A.W. Nichols is growing better. Though its ranks have been greatly thinned by casualties, it is considered one of the reliable regiments."[471]

In the early morning hours of April 2, 1865, a general demonstration upon the Confederate works was ordered, and the First Michigan Sharpshooters, under the command of Major Nichols, crept out of the Union lines and beyond the trenches and approached the Confederate works. Upon Nichols's command, "'Forward, all. On the run—go on quick'...with a shout the whole line rose and charged....Nichols exhorted his men onward. Sword upraised, he fell over the embankment with a bullet in his side."[472] Although their attack successfully gained a portion of the Confederate trenches, it was not supported, and the regiment was forced to fall back to its own lines with its wounded, including its severely wounded commanding officer. The following morning, the regiment was ordered to attack the same Confederate works, and this time it found the line deserted, as the Confederates had evacuated Petersburg. The flag of the First Michigan Sharpshooters was the first Union flag to fly over the evacuated and surrendered city, and all knew this signaled the beginning of the end for the Confederacy. Only six days later, Confederate general Robert E. Lee surrendered his army at Appomattox Court House, Virginia.

By June, Nichols, who had received the brevet rank of colonel in recognition of his bravery in the attack at Petersburg, was home again on furlough, attempting to recuperate from his severe wounding. Shortly after the disbanding of his regiment, he moved his wife, Sarah, and two children to D.C., where he had accepted a position as clerk in the Treasury Department. The pain from his wound, however, was his constant companion, and in

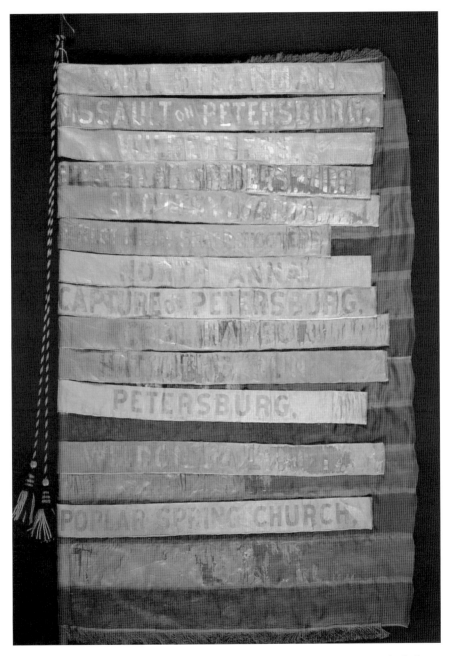

Battle flag of the First Michigan Sharpshooters Regiment, with battle streamers, including "First Flag over Petersburg." *Save the Flags.*

On the east side of the Sharpshooters monument on the grounds of the state capitol are inscribed in memory the names Asahel Nichols and Henry Hinkley. *Michigan State Capitol Collection, David Marvin.*

January, he returned alone to Lansing and stayed with his brother-in-law, feeling a change of climate might help him recover. His condition worsened, however, as he suffered debilitating headaches and episodes of delirium; his brother-in-law found him one evening standing in his bedroom "fighting rebels." Nichols seemed to rally and requested the ammunition for his revolver be returned to him in preparation for his return to D.C., explaining that he never traveled without the loaded weapon. On the morning of January 18, Colonel Asahel Nichols put that loaded pistol to his right temple and pulled the trigger, ending the pain and torment of his young life. He was twenty-eight. "He was a brave soldier, a good citizen, an honorable high-minded man, he lived honored and died regretted."[473]

Two years later, while living in the Lansing home of Nichols's widow, Sarah, Sarah's brother Henry Hinckley was also suffering from the effects of his service. Unable to work due to illness, he stated "he had not seen a well hour since a shell had burst close to his head."[474] After unsuccessfully attempting to retrieve the weapon his brother-in-law had used to end his life, Hinckley was able to procure a loaded pistol, and in his bedroom in his sister's home, on the evening of March 31, 1868, he, too, ended his tormented life by a self-inflicted shot to the head.

These two boys from Lansing who rose through the ranks to become regimental officers, one a brevet colonel and the other a captain, survived the war and came home to their families and a well-deserved hero's welcome. Sadly, the physical and mental pain, survivor's guilt and what is now commonly known as post-traumatic stress were their constant companions. Seeking out treatment or even admitting to the need for help would have been virtually unheard-of at the time, so these two men suffered their pain largely in silence. These two young men who had left Lansing as bright-eyed, optimistic, patriotic volunteers and had become brothers-in-arms and brothers-in-law eventually took their own lives in their effort to finally end that pain. They were two of the all too many postwar casualties, men who succumbed to their mental anguish and to their physical injuries well after the last angry shots had been fired.

Chapter 17

MY BOY'S NOT COMING HOME

The Thing I Feared Is Come

On Palm Sunday, April 9, 1865, General Robert E. Lee surrendered his Confederate Army of Northern Virginia to Union general Ulysses S. Grant at Appomattox Court House, Virginia. Within weeks, other Confederate armies would also surrender, finally bringing to an end the national nightmare that was the Civil War. The celebration of the end of the war was, however, quickly muted by the assassination of President Abraham Lincoln on Good Friday, April 14. When word of the assassination reached Lansing by telegraph early the following morning, it was thought by many that it was a mistake, but when details flowed in, the sad truth was apparent. A crowd gathered around the telegraph office, and a meeting was called at the statehouse that afternoon. All business was suspended; the bells of the churches and schools tolled for two hours; all the flags were immediately put at half-staff and public buildings draped in black. At three o'clock in the afternoon, a large group of citizens met at the capitol to pray and to hear a number of resolutions that had been prepared, led by Lansing mayor I.H. Bartholomew and the Reverend Edward Meyer.[475]

On the following Wednesday, Lansing held a funeral rite for the slain president including, a procession through town and a service in the House of Representatives. Participating in the event were the owners of Lansing businesses from Lower, Middle and Upper Town, members of the Common Council and elected officials including the mayor and the state officers and employees. The city band led the melancholy parade of citizens, composed of the fire departments; the ladies from the Female College; students from the

Agricultural College, the Boys' Reform School and the Lansing Academy; the Masons; and the public school students and teachers. Among the most distinguished guests were the numerous maimed and discharged soldiers and officers already returned from the battlefield, those who had answered "Father Abraham's" call.[476] In sympathetic appreciation for the sad affair, a cleansing, warm springtime rain fell upon the gathered crowd, as if to wash away the tears, the turmoil and the blood of the last four years.

In early June 1865, a poem by William Cullen Bryant titled "Our Boys Are Coming Home" ran in the *Republican*: "Thank God the sky is clearing.… Soon shall the joy bells ringing…but now our prayers are granted, Our boys are coming home."[477] Two weeks later, in response, another poem, authored by the Reverend Edward Meyer of Lansing's St. Paul's Episcopal Church, appeared. Meyer's son Henry was killed in action at Antietam. His poem was titled "My Boy's Not Coming Home." "The thought shall shroud and sadden…the bonfires sadly gleam.…The thing I feared is come.…Antietam's grasses are springing o'er his grave.…My Boy's Not Coming Home."[478]

In a letter to his sister in late 1864, Theodore Foster wrote, "The brave boys go from the same communities and die in places far apart from each other.…I have given my best abilities during this campaign, in my little place, to do what I could against the great curse of my country, and if I should see it blotted out before I die, it would be much more than, in former years, I could ever had hoped for."[479] A few short months after the end of the war, two days past Christmas, on December 27, 1865, Theodore Foster, at home in Lansing, died of the effects of his long battle with consumption.

One year after the conclusion of the war, an article appeared in the *Republican* listing the parameters of the newly passed pension law that was highly pertinent to numerous Lansing veterans and their families and encompassed, perhaps better than any other description, the very human costs of man's folly of war. The loss of both eyes, both hands or the use of the latter equaled twenty-five dollars per month; the loss of both feet, one hand and one foot or the use of same equaled twenty dollars per month; loss of one foot or one hand was valued at fifteen dollars per month.[480] How it is possible to place a monetary value on such staggering loss beggars the imagination.

The men returned to their Lansing homes determined that what they had seen and done should actually mean something, that it should not be frittered away and wasted. That it should go toward building a state and a new nation that was truly worthy of their service and sacrifice, a state and a free nation that, by God, was truly worthy of the buckets of blood that had

Civil War amputees playing croquet on the grounds of the State Office Building in Lansing. *Forest Parke Library and Archives, Capital Area District Library.*

been spilled. They were also determined that they should be remembered, not in some boastful or vainglorious attempt at immortality but with the desire, the hope, the fervent prayer that the madness, the uselessness, the horrible utter brutality that is all war would never, ever again be visited on this nation, on their progeny, their children or their children's children. So it is that we proceed today, rather futilely attempting to keep their fervent prayer alive.

Each man went home with the unstated question left unanswered: How does a returning soldier pick up the pieces of a life abandoned four years earlier, taking to his domicile the memories of horrendous sights, sounds and actions better left deeply buried and unspoken? The soldiers carried home with them the weighty, unbearable burden of the guilt of Cain for having slain his own brother. They also carried with them the perhaps even

Monument to Lansing's Civil War veterans at Mt. Hope Cemetery. *Michigan State Capitol Collection, David Marvin.*

heavier burden of their mere and yet most audacious act of survival while so many comrades and boyhood friends perished round and about them in the struggle. How does a former soldier, in his newly reclaimed daily life of a citizen, face the parents, wives and children of friends buried in their blood-soaked uniforms in shallow, hastily dug graves so far away from the great shores of Michigan and the quiet, peaceful streets of Lansing?

Appendix

Roster of Lansing Soldiers

In 1882, John Robertson, who served as Michigan's adjutant general from 1861 to his death in 1887, published his monumental book, *Michigan in the War*. The over-one-thousand-page volume was ordered and commissioned by the state legislature and included histories of all the Michigan regiments, batteries and units that participated in the Civil War. The book also included a register of commissioned officers and a short summary of their individual service.

General Robertson's work was well received, but many enlisted men felt their contributions and sacrifices had not been appropriately included and recorded for posterity. By Legislative Act 147 of 1903, Adjutant General George Brown was ordered to compile and publish, along with the capable assistance of his clerks—some of whom were veterans of the war—a history of each individual unit and short summaries of the service of each volunteer and drafted man who had served in the war of the rebellion. What is commonly known by Civil War researchers and historians as the "Brown Books," a reference both to Adjutant General Brown and the actual color of the books' bindings, eventually numbered forty-six volumes. The following list of Lansing men who fought in the war is drawn from the Brown Books, *Record of Service of Michigan Volunteers in the Civil War, 1861–1865*.

This roster includes all men who reported Lansing as their primary residence at the time of their enlistment and includes men who enlisted at Lansing while their primary residence may have been another town or city. Included also are men who listed Ingham County as their place of residence, if proof could be found from draft registrations or census data from 1860 that Lansing was their primary residence at the time of their enlistment. The list does not include men who settled in Lansing postwar. In some cases, soldiers are included in this list if other documents prove they did in fact reside in Lansing but neglected to list it as their residence. Some soldiers may appear on several lists if they fought with multiple regiments. The author does not purport the list to be comprehensive and apologizes for any inadvertent omissions.

MICHIGAN VOLUNTEER INFANTRY REGIMENTS

FIRST (THREE MONTHS AND THREE YEARS)

James Bell, James Bennett, Alpheus Bixby, Andrew Briggs, Thomas Burrows, John De Forest, Avalma Dickinson, Azariah Ege, Rudolph (aka Randall) Hoffman, James Marsh, William Melville, Edward Meyer, George Meyer, Alonzo Northrop, Peter Quinn, Joseph Saaxa, John Saltmarsh, Levi Soule, John Wyman

SECOND

Elijah Lareau, Adolphus Williams

THIRD

William Agard, Samuel Alexander, James Ballard, John Broad, Thomas Butler, Albert Carr, William Choates, Charles Clark, Edgar Clark, Richard Cottrell, Lawrence Croy, James Dalton, John Elliott, George Ellis, Charles Foster, William Hogan, Robert Jefferds, George Johnson, Michael Kane, Riley Kent, Stephen Longyear, Ira Lyon, Henry Mange, Edward Marsh, Joseph Mason, Andrew Miller, Charles Price, John Price, George Randall, Charles Schasberger, Allen Shattuck, Daniel Shattuck, Nelson Shattuck, Eli Siverd, Joseph Stevens, James Ten Eyck, Jerome Ten Eyck, Homer Thayer, Ira Turner, David Webb

FOURTH

Elijah Laverty

FIFTH
Alanson Dean

SIXTH
Thomas Rourke

EIGHTH
Elijah Allen, John Baker, Franklin Baldwin, Samuel Baldwin, Martin Beebe, Edwin Benson, Henry Buck, John Burgoyne, Franklin H. Burnham, John Campbell, Henry Chadwick, James (aka George) Chaffee, George Chandler, Nelson Chapman, Abraham Cottrell, Farrel Cowley, Albert Crawford, John Davidson, James Davis, Andrew Deitz, James Dillabaugh, John Elder, Matthew Elder, Jabez Elkins, William Ellis, Lyman Elwood, Nathan (aka Matthew) Everett, William Farley, Matthew Fitzpatrick, Edward Flower, Dorman Fuller, John Fuller, Robert A. Fulton (aka Fuller), James Gordon (aka Gorgan), Michael Halick, John Hall, William Harback, Elisha Harrington, Cornelius Haviland, Ransom Howe, Lyman Hull, Sibley Ingersoll, Cephas Johnson, Colonel Johnson, Francis Johnson, Charles Junette (aka Jonette), Edward Light, Thomas Little, William Longstreet, Wesley McCave, Marcus McCrumb, Orren Moore, Hartwell Nichols, Judson Painly (aka Pinny), Wilbert Palmenter, Robert Patrick, Thomas Perry, Peter Portney (aka Poutney), Henry Pulver, Hulbert Shank, Edgar Shattuck, John Sheets, Frederick Shipp, Daniel Stafford, John Surato, Amos Teman, Heman Throop, George Truce, Charles Turrell, Frederick Turrell, Andrew Vanlooven, John Wells, Henry Wightman, Henry Wilber, Luther Winters, Daniel Wiser

NINTH
William Beal, George Brown, Richard Graham, Erastus Kimbeck, David Longborn, John Russell

TENTH
Abram Savage

TWELFTH

Peter Braban, Isaac Cravath, Daniel Ellis, Edwin (aka Edward) Foster, George Gassimere, William Gibson, Peter Gieffer, Henry Guest, John Hetzel, Edward Hinman, Harmon Hulse, Robert Kedzie, Thomas Kenyon, John Kuhnle, Jerome Lafferty, James Marble, Thomas McCurdy, Albert Mosher, John Nagel, Harrison Nash, John M. Newsom, John Oatley, William Oatley, George Parker, Charles Riley, David Schaible, John Schleicher, James Secord, John Seitzie (aka Seising), Albert Sherman, John Strong, Edward Underhill, John Wardell, Joseph Wardell, Edward Yauger (aka Yawger)

THIRTEENTH

William Foster

FOURTEENTH

Merrit Adams, Cyrus Alsdorf, Henry Alward, Sylvanus Bachelder, Alpheus Beebe, Howard Beebe, James Bishop, Samuel Blackman, Michael Brown, Charles Bush, James Dearing, James Dixon, John Dorr, Hiram Griffin, Charles Haner, Charles Hinman, Daniel Hinman, Francis Holly, Theodore Holmes, James Jeffries, Augustus Jeyte, George Karn, Nelson Lewis, William Little, William McCue, Patrick McManamon, Daniel Mevis, Nicholas Middleton, James Morgan, Patrick Mulvany, Abel Myers, Joseph Myers, Elmer North, Henry Petty, Samuel Rogers, George Root, George Severance, James Tetter, James Van Dyke, Alexander Wolcott

SIXTEENTH

Henry Beard, Alexander Cameron, John Dake, James Eggleston, James Enslan, John Gardner, Nathan Severance, James Vanarsdall, Jacob Weber (aka Webber)

SEVENTEENTH

Isaac Colvin, Bruno De Ruth, Sylvester Evarts, Charles Farrand, William Jordan, Uriah Lazelle, Ephrain Meacham, Henry Meyer, William Robson, Alonzo Stevens, Henry Warner

TWENTIETH

Andrew Adams, Henry Baker, William Barnard, Benjamin Berry, Hiram Beeman, Henry Bignal, LeRoy Boice, Malcolm Boileau, Addison Boyce, Norman Brooks, Tillinghast Brownell, James Buel, Ichabod Burdick, Ranselas Burlingame, Darius Calkins, William Calkins, Harrison Call, Henry Carpenter, George Cheney, Orville Chubb, Cyrus Coryell, Albert Cowles, Thomas Cronk, James Dermott, John Douglas, Thomas Douglas, Wilber DuBois, Arthur Edwards, James Evens, Elihu Filer, Daniel Fisher, John Fuller, Latham Garlick, Jermain Gilson, William Greene, John Hailstone, James Haviland, Williams Higgins, Henry Hinckley, Andrew Honey, Albert Hudson, Edwin Hudson, Herbert Hudson, Leonard Hull, George Humphrey, Lafayette Hutt, Nicholas Ikenburg, George Jimmerson, Jerome Kroll, Lloyd Lewis, Julian Love, Andrew Morehouse, Stephen Morehouse, Thomas Morehouse, Elisha Mosher, Jeremiah O'Brien, Harmon Paddleford, William Raynor, Leonard Rice, Horace Rogers, Francis Rowley, Martin Ryan, Schuyler Seager, George Seymour, Jacob Siebert, Anthony Sitser, James Slocum, Frazer Smalley, John Smith, Martin Smith, Milo Smith, William Huntington Smith, William Squires, Augustus Stevens, George Strickland, William Tallman, Nathaniel Thayer, Horace Turner, Christian Wakenhut, James Ward, Roderick Wheeler, Adolphus Williams

TWENTY-FIRST
Edward Baker

TWENTY-SECOND
William Sanborn

TWENTY-THIRD
Andrew Pettengill

TWENTY-FOURTH
Charles Rheu

Twenty-Sixth
Napoleon De Long, Henry Hawley

Twenty-Eighth
John Agen, George Angel, Joseph Beaumont, Edson Boswell, Danford Briggs, William Cary, Alfred Chapman, George Cook, John Cook, Homer Cornell, John Kennedy, William Kent, George Lapham, Henry Maxfield, George Montgomery, Cornelius Myers, Nelson Purdy, Melville Roberts, Henry Sanders, Edward Sherridan, Isaac Sloan, Luther Stone, Abraham Wager, Charles Williams, William Woods

Twenty-Ninth
Alpheus Beebe, Thomas Carrigan

Thirtieth
Ambrose Arnold, George Ayres, Ragan Baker, Elijah Baldwin, Benjamin Bell, Andrew Call, Sam Champlin, Henry Cutler, Darwin Donaldson, Stephen Drum, Smith Hall, John Hubbard, Albert Jones, Andrew Jones, George Limeback, Charles Myers, Henry Powell, Henry Rouse, Frank Torrence

Michigan Volunteer Cavalry Regiments

First
Alpheus Carr, Henry Duchine, Rice Eddy, Louis (aka Lewis) Godfrey, Herman Hascall, Morris Hobbs, Henry Hunt, David Johnson, Amos McClure, Lorenzo Poor(e), Albert Rush, Andrew Steadman, Daniel (aka David) Tanner, William Thompson, Squire Waters

Third
Lester Bond, Elias Fulmer, George Lathrop, Elmer Miller, Cassius Stafford, Leonidas Whitman

FOURTH
Chester Armstrong, John Bacon, John Chadwick, William Kenyon, Franklin Leach, Patrick Ryan, Peter Supry

FIFTH
Albert Crane, Adam Straub

SIXTH
Samuel Bloomburg, George Bugsbee, George Clark, Edward Harlock, Reuben Heath, Milo Hopkins, Henry Lewis, William Lewis, Nelson Madden, Peter McLane, Charles Mears, Judson Miller, Merritt Miller, Henry Norton, Daniel Parker, James Pease, Martin Phelps, Frederick Richardson, Hiram Rix, Horace Rogers, Charles Rulison, Clark Scammon, Samuel Scammon, Schuyler Seager, Willis Shaw, James Somerville, John Tooker, William Torrance, George Tucker

SEVENTH
William Adams, Charles McClelland, Tracy Merrell, William Wait

NINTH
Patrick Sullivan

TENTH
Bradford Elderkin, Alonzo Handy, Thomas Kenyon, George Madden, Emanuel Scott, Jacob VanHusen, Willam Woodruff

ELEVENTH
Charles Adams, Albert Baker, Julius Baker, Henry Clark, Charles Foster, John Fullmore, Harvey Huxley, John Johnson, Lawson Lee, Thomas Little, Ezra Marsh, Charles Reynolds, Andrew Shelden, James Ward

FIRST MICHIGAN ENGINEERS AND MECHANICS REGIMENT

Benjamin Church, William Gavett, Silas Hastings, Gilbert Hasty, William Hunter, Joseph Smith

FIRST MICHIGAN LIGHT ARTILLERY REGIMENT

Amasa Place (Battery B), Daniel Campbell (Battery G)

FIRST MICHIGAN VOLUNTEER COLORED INFANTRY REGIMENT/102ND USCT

Benjamin Brooks, Benjamin Cooper, Charles Crockett, Benjamin Green, William Harrison, Noah Hill, William Howard, George Morgan, Charles Points

FIRST MICHIGAN VOLUNTEER SHARPSHOOTERS REGIMENT

Marshal Adams, John Anderson, Henry Barnes, Robert Bartlett, Mark Child, William Cooper, Henry Hinckley, Joseph Kilbourn, John McGiveron, Asahel Nichols, George (aka Eli H.) Nichols, James Sharkey

UNITED STATES FEDERAL UNITS

FIRST UNITED STATES SHARPSHOOTERS REGIMENT

Albert Baker, James Baker, Alonzo Ballard, James Dillabaugh, Jacob Ege, Henry Gilchrist, Edward Hamilton, William Jackson, Johnson Robinson, Asa Shattuck, Daniel Shattuck, Peter Van Etter, John Wiser

SECOND UNITED STATES SHARPSHOOTERS REGIMENT

Edward Adams, Oscar Baker, Henry Ballard, Emerson Bartlett, John Bohnet, Jeremiah Brown, Darius Calkins, Orrin Case, George Cole, William Denny, Joseph Elder, Daniel Ellis, John Ellis, Thomas Ellis, Hiram Enslen, Welton Fitts, Charles Foster, Seymour Foster, Benjamin Goodhue, Wilber Howard, Albert Hulsapple, Charles Hunt, George Morton, Morris Norton, William Ostrom, Henry Parker, Martin Phelps, Sylvanus Piersons, William Sherwood, Andrew Stuart, Ulysses Ward, John Whitman, William Wilcox

Seventeenth U.S. Infantry
E.R. Merrifield

United States Navy
Asa Winter

United States Paymaster Volunteers
Daniel Case

Units from Other States

1st Battalion, First Ohio Sharpshooters Regiment
Joseph Hull

1st Indiana Light Artillery Battery
M.C. Skinner

9th Illinois Cavalry
George Smith

26th New York Infantry
I. Van Huesen

102nd New York Infantry
Daniel Case

142nd Illinois Infantry Regiment
Charles Bryant

148th New York Infantry
Rush Shank

Notes

Introduction

1. "The Naming of the Charles T. Foster Post G.A.R.," *Michigan History Magazine*, vol. 9 (1925): 149.
2. "Allan S. Shattuck Climbed Capitol Dome 36 Years Ago," *State Journal*, October 6, 1916 (hereafter *Journal*).
3. Demographia, "US Population History."
4. "Pioneer Times at North End," *Lansing State Republican*, May 9, 1905 (hereafter *Republican*). Accessed via www.newspapers.com.
5. Lawler, "Origin."
6. Edmonds, *Early Lansing History*, 12–21.
7. "Detroit, Kalamazoo, and Lansing," *Republican*, September 19, 1860.
8. "Ohio and Michigan," *Republican*, September 19, 1860.
9. "Shameful," *Republican*, January 14, 1863.
10. Ibid.

Chapter 1

11. "Citizens' Meeting," *Republican*, April 24, 1861.
12. *Michigan History Magazine* 9, 143–49.
13. Ibid.
14. "Theodore Foster," *Republican*, January 3, 1866; Foster, *Some Michigan Descendants*, 87.

15. "The Jackson Encampment," *Republican*, August 15, 1860.

16. "William's Rifles," *Republican*, May 8, 1861.

17. "1860 Lansing Census," *Republican*, January 5, 1889; Michigan Adjutant-General's Department, *Record of Service*, vols. 44 (131), 3 (100) and 8 (131).

18. United States Federal Census, 1860, Lansing.

19. Castro, "The Man Who Died Twice," 33–36.

20. "John Broad, Civil War Veteran 'Killed' In Battle of Fair Oaks, Succumbs," *Journal*, September 4, 1915.

21. Siverd, Frank, "Stray Leaves from Camp—No. 10," *Republican*, August 14, 1861.

22. "A Disgraceful Affair," *Republican*, July 3, 1861; Michigan Adjutant-General's Department, *Record of Service*, vol. 3, 91.

23. *Veteran* (Save the Flags Records, Third Michigan Binder, 1884), 300.

24. Michigan Department of Transportation, "Michigan's Railroad History," 8.

25. Robertson, John. *Michigan in the War*. Lansing: W.S. George, 1882., p 206. (hereafter Robertson)

26. Garret Ellison, "Remembering the 1,040-Man West Michigan Regiment Who Fought in the Civil War 150 Years Ago." MLive, April 3, 2019.

27. "A Specimen Brick," *Republican*, May 22, 1861.

28. Siverd, Frank, "Stray Leaves from Camp—No. 1," *Republican*, May 29, 1861.

29. Siverd, Frank, "Stray Leaves from Camp—No. 2," *Republican*, June 5, 1861.

30. Siverd, Frank, "Stray Leaves from Camp—No. 1," *Republican*, May 29, 1861.

31. "Presentation of the Flag to the Third Regiment," *Grand Rapids Enquirer*, June 5, 1861.

32. "Departure of the Third Regiment," *Grand Rapids Daily Eagle*, June 13, 1861.

33. "Arrival of The Third Regiment," *Detroit Advertiser and Tribune*, June 14, 1861.

Chapter 2

34. Cowles, Albert E. *Past and Present of the City of Lansing and Ingham County, Michigan*. Lansing: Michigan Historical Publishing Association, 1905. p. 56.

35. "City Improvements," *Republican*, September 19, 1860.

36. "What We Are About in Lansing," *Republican*, August 9, 1859.

37. "Mr. Editor," *Republican*, July 23, 1862.

38. "City Council," *Republican*, August 14, 1865.

39. "The New Bridge," *Republican*, January 13, 1864.

40. "Churches," *Republican*, May 7, 1862.

41. Ibid.

42. "Lansing City Religious Directory," *Republican*, January 9, 1861.

43. "Universalist Church," *Republican*, September 16, 1863.

44. "Catholic Church," *Republican*, August 17, 1864; "The Catholic Church," November 23, 1864; "Catholic Church," February 22, 1865.

45. "Universalist Church," *Republican*, September 16, 1863.

46. "The City School Census," *Republican*, August 30, 1865.

47. "The Public Schools," *Republican*, April 5, 1865.

48. "History of Lansing Hotels Traced from Days of Coach," *Journal*, February 8, 1930.

49. "A Card," *Republican*, July 20, 1864.

50. "Fire at the Reform School," *Republican*, October 30, 1861.

51. Clark, *Michigan State Gazetteer*, 374–78.

52. *Republican*, August 13, 1862.

53. United States Federal Census, 1860, Lansing.

54. "Whitney the Magician," *Republican*, January 11, 1865.

55. "Sleighing," *Republican*, December 12, 1860.

56. Adam, Mrs. Franc L. *The Pioneer History of Ingham County*. Vol. 1. Lansing, MI: Wynkoop, Hallenbeck, Crawford, 1923. 479.

57. "New Years at Lansing," *Republican*, January 3, 1860.

58. Ibid.

59. "Lower Town Items," *Republican*, August 8, 1866.

60. Public Act 17, *Michigan Compiled Laws*. University of Michigan, 1855.

61. Clark, *Michigan State Gazetteer*, 374–78.

62. "Mobocracy," *Republican*, July 5, 1865.

Chapter 3

63. Siverd, Frank, "Stray Leaves from Camp—No. 4," *Republican*, June 26, 1861.

64. Siverd, Frank, "Stray Leaves from Camp—No. 6," *Republican*, July 17, 1861.

65. Siverd, Frank, "Stray Leaves from Camp—No. 5," *Republican*, July 10, 1861.

66. Siverd, Frank, "Stray Leaves from Camp—No. 6," *Republican*, July 5, 1861.

67. United States War Department et al., War of the Rebellion, 373–77.

68. Siverd, Frank, "Stray Leaves from Camp—No. 9," *Republican*, July 31, 1861.

69. *Republican*, June 18, 1862.

70. "Returned," *Republican*, August 7, 1861.

71. Siverd, Frank, "Stray Leaves from Camp—No. 11," *Republican*, August 21, 1861.

72. Siverd, Frank, "Stray Leaves from Camp—No. 12," *Republican*, September 18, 1861.

73. Ibid.

74. Siverd, Frank, "Stray Leaves from Camp—No. 13," *Republican*, October 16, 1861.

75. Siverd, Frank, "Stray Leaves from Camp—No. 14," *Republican*, December 11, 1861.

76. Siverd, Frank, "Stray Leaves from Camp No. 15," *Republican*, January 8, 1862.

77. Ibid.

78. Siverd, Frank, "Stray Leaves from Camp—No. 16," *Republican*, March 5, 1862.

79. Siverd, Frank, "Stray Leaves from Camp—No. 18," *Republican*, April 30, 1862.

80. Ibid.

81. Siverd, Frank, "Stray Leaves from Camp—No. 20," *Republican*, May 21, 1862.

82. "Naming," 149.

83. Ibid.

84. *Republican*, May 21, 1862.

85. "Naming," 148.

86. Ibid., 149.

87. Foster, *Descendants of Theodore Foster*, 87.

88. Ibid., 89.

89. Roosevelt, "Very Sad Thing."

90. Thayer, Homer, "Letters from the Michigan 3rd Regiment," *Republican*, June 18, 1862.

91. Ibid.

92. Ibid.

93. *Records of Internment.*

94. "A Deserved Tribute," *Republican*, June 17, 1863.

95. "John Broad, Civil War Veteran 'Killed' In Battle of Fair Oaks, Succumbs," *Journal*, September 4, 1915.

96. "Our Gallant Third Regiment," *Republican*, August 6, 1862.

97. "Death After Day's Illness: Michael Kane of This City Had a Fine Civil War Record," *Republican*, June 14, 1910.

98. Robertson, *Michigan in the War*, 214.

99. "Death After Day's Illness: Michael Kane of This City Had a Fine Civil War Record," *Republican*, June 14, 1910.

100. "From the Third Michigan Regiment," *Republican*, May 20, 1863.

101. "Casualties," *Republican*, May 13, 1863.

102. "Married," *Republican*, September 9, 1863.

103. *Portrait and Biographical Album of Ingham and Livingston Counties*, 675–79.

104. "Bounties for the Third Regiment," *Republican*, March 23, 1864.

105. "Veteran Returned," *Republican*, October 5, 1864.

106. *Michigan, U.S., Death Records, 1867–1952.*

107. Robertson, *Michigan in the War*, 216.

108. "Allan S. Shattuck Climbed Capitol Dome 36 Years Ago," *Journal*, October 6, 1916.

109. "The Old Third," *Republican*, September 28, 1864.

110. "Return of the Fifth Regiment," *Republican*, July 26, 1865.

Chapter 4

111. "The News," *Republican*, February 13, 1861.

112. Barnett, "Sample Michigan Land Grant," 1–28.

113. Daboll and Kelley, *Clinton County, Michigan*, 464.

114. Elliott, "Transportation in Lansing," 9.

115. "The Railroad," *Republican*, April 12, 1859.

116. Hoffman, *My Brave Mechanics*, 4.

117. Army Jr., *Engineering Victory*, 86.

118. Hoffman, *My Brave Mechanics*, 11.

119. Michigan Adjutant-General's Department, *Record of Service*, vol. 43.

120. "Engineers and Mechanics," *Republican*, March 25, 1863.

121. United States Federal Census, 1860, Lansing.

122. "Another Fallen," *Republican*, July 29, 1863.

123. "Amboy, Lansing and Grand Traverse Bay Railroad," *Republican*, December 18, 1861.
124. "Rams Horn Railroad," *Republican*, April 2, 1862.
125. "The Ram's Horn Again," *Republican*, May 21, 1862.
126. "The Railroad," *Republican*, August 6, 1862.
127. "The Ram's Horn," *Republican*, October 29, 1862.
128. "The Railroad," *Republican*, November 5, 1862.
129. "A Telegraph Line," *Republican*, January 7, 1863.
130. Bingham, *Michigan Biographies*, vol. 2, 32.
131. "Telegraph from Owosso to Lansing," *Republican*, January 21, 1863.
132. "Telegraph to Owosso," *Republican*, September 9, 1863; "Telegraphic," *Republican*, October 14, 1863.
133. "Telegraph," *Republican*, December 16, 1863.
134. "The Telegraph," *Republican*, January 13, 1864.

Chapter 5

135. Stevens, *Berdan's*, 2.
136. Robertson, *Michigan in the War*, 119.
137. Ibid., 119.
138. "Attention Sharpshooters," *Republican*, July 24, 1861.
139. United States Federal Census, 1850, Madison Township.
140. Michigan Pioneer and Historical Society, *Historical Collections*, vol. 38, 679–80.
141. United States Federal Census, 1860, Lansing, 49.
142. Tinder, *Directory of Early Photographers*.
143. Baker, Berdan's Rifle Corps of Sharpshooters, Certificate of Marksmanship.
144. Michigan Adjutant-General's Department, *Record of Service*, vol. 41, 8.
145. Ibid., vol. 44, 107.
146. "Sharpshooters," *Republican*, August 21, 1861.
147. "Gone to Camp," *Republican*, July 17, 1861.
148. "Annual Election," *Republican*, October 25, 1859.
149. "Election of Officers of the Fire Department," *Republican*, June 12, 1861.
150. "I.O.O.F.," *Republican*, May 23, 1860.
151. "Delegates to the County Convention," *Republican*, March 13, 1860.
152. "Lincoln Wide Awake Club," *Republican*, June 13, 1860.

153. "Death of Lieut. J.J. Whitman," *Republican*, October 1, 1862.

154. "Was He a PostMaster?" *Republican*, September 12, 1860.

155. Whitman, "Last Will and Testament."

156. United States Federal Census, 1860, Lansing.

157. "A Pistol to Lieut. D. Calkins," *Republican*, October 2, 1861.

158. "Presentation to Lieut. J.J. Whitman," *Republican*, October 2, 1861.

159. Ibid.

160. United States Federal Census, 1860, Lansing.

161. "Republican Pets," *Republican*, March 16, 1864.

162. "The Sharp-Shooters," *Republican*, August 28, 1861.

163. "Correspondence of the Republican," *Republican*, October 16, 1861.

164. Ibid.

165. "From Stuart's Sharpshooters," *Republican*, November 6, 1861.

166. Ibid.

167. "Berdan Sharp Shooters," *Republican*, October 9, 1861.

168. "From Stuart's Sharpshooters," *Republican*, November 20, 1861.

169. Ibid.

170. Michigan Adjutant-General's Department, *Record of Service*, vol. 45, 324.

171. United States Federal Census, 1860, Lansing.

172. "Personal," *Republican*, July 9, 1862.

173. "From Stuart's Sharpshooters," *Republican*, November 20, 1861.

174. "From the Wolverine Sharp-Shooters," *Republican*, December 4, 1861.

175. Ibid.

176. "From the Wolverine Sharp-Shooters," *Republican*, December 25, 1861.

177. Ibid.

178. Ibid.

179. "Arms for Berdan's Sharp Shooters," *Republican*, January 8, 1862.

180. *Life*, "History of the Rifle," 62–63.

181. "From the Wolverine Sharpshooters," *Republican*, January 15, 1862.

182. Ibid.

183. Stevens, *Berdan's*, 16.

184. "From the Wolverine Sharpshooters," *Republican*, January 15, 1862.

185. Ibid.

186. Ibid.

187. Ibid.

188. Ibid.

189. Michigan, U.S., County Marriage Records, 1822–1940, Ancestry.com.

190. "On a Furlough," *Republican*, March 5, 1862.
191. "The Sharp Shooters," *Republican*, February 26, 1862.
192. "Lieut. Calkins," *Republican*, April 30, 1862.
193. "The Sharp Shooters," *Republican*, February 26, 1862.
194. "In Town," *Republican*, March 12, 1862.
195. Baker, personal notebook.

Chapter 6

196. *Republican*, April 24, 1861.
197. Wilbur, *Civil War Medicine*, 17.
198. Stille, *History of the United States Sanitary Commission*, 63.
199. Seidman, "We Were Enlisted," 61.
200. "Number of Families," *Republican*, November 6, 1861.
201. "A Card," *Republican*, July 24, 1861.
202. "Appeal to Patriotic Women," *Republican*, October 30, 1861.
203. Michigan Pioneer and Historical Society, *Historical Collections*, vol. 4, 11–12.
204. "H.R. Pratt, Former State Official Dies," *Journal*, December 9, 1915.
205. United States Federal Census, 1860, Lansing.
206. Michigan Adjutant-General's Department, *Record of Service*, vol. 34, 8.
207. "Off to the War," *Republican*, April 13, 1864.
208. "Dr. J.B. Hull," *Republican*, May 20, 1901.
209. "Military Aid Society," *Republican*, November 12, 1862.
210. "Important to the Friends of Michigan Soldiers," *Republican*, December 24, 1862.
211. "Eighth Regt. Mich. Infantry, Vol's," *Republican*, December 10, 1862.
212. "From Beaufort, S.C.," *Republican*, March 19, 1862.
213. "Correspondence from Florida," *Republican*, October 29, 1862.
214. Bagley Family Papers.
215. "Naval Correspondence," *Republican*, August 10, 1864.
216. "The Ladies Military Aid Society," *Republican*, October 15, 1862.
217. "Encouragement for Well Doing," *Republican*, January 28, 1863.
218. "How to Support the Government," *Republican*, August 19, 1863.
219. "Ladies Loyal League," *Republican*, September 2, 1863.
220. Foster, *Descendants of Theodore Foster*, 119–20.
221. "Donations to the Sanitary Fair at Chicago," *Republican*, November 11, 1863.

222. "The Freedmen's Fair," *Republican*, March 1, 1865.
223. Michigan Pioneer and Historical Society, *Historical Collections*, vol. 17 (Lansing, MI: W.S. George and Co. State Printers, 1892) 101.
224. Seidman, "We Were Enlisted," 61.
225. Tomek, "Women and Soldiers' Aid Societies," 11.

Chapter 7

226. "Correspondence of the Lansing Republican," *Republican*, April 23, 1862.
227. Ibid.
228. Ibid.
229. "From the Wolverine Sharp-Shooters," *Republican*, June 18, 1862.
230. Baker, personal notebook.
231. Ibid.
232. "Letter from Lieut. Baker," *Republican*, July 16, 1862.
233. Ibid.
234. Ibid.
235. Dempsey and Egen, *Michigan at Antietam*, 9.
236. Stevens, *Berdan's*, 202.
237. "Letter from F.G. Russell," *Republican*, October 22, 1862.
238. United States Federal Census, 1860, Lansing.
239. "Letter from F.G. Russell."
240. Michigan Adjutant-General's Department, *Record of Service*, vol. 3, 75.
241. "Died," *Republican*, October 8, 1862.
242. "A Soldier's Funeral," *Republican*, October 15, 1862.
243. Baker, personal notebook.
244. "Promotion," *Republican*, November 26, 1862.
245. "Sword Presentation," *Republican*, February 25, 1863.
246. "From the 2nd Regt. U.S. Sharp Shooters," *Republican*, May 28, 1863.
247. Michigan Adjutant-General's Department, *Record of Service*, vol. 44, 137.
248. "Casualties," *Republican*, May 13, 1863.
249. Stevens, *Berdan's*, 315.
250. Ibid., 317.
251. "Arrival of Sharp Shooters," *Republican*, January 20, 1864.
252. "U.S. Sharp-Shooters," *Republican*, February 24, 1864.
253. "From the 2nd Regt. U.S. Sharp Shooters," *Republican*, June 22, 1864.

254. Michigan Adjutant-General's Department, *Record of Service*, vol. 44, 110.
255. "Second U.S. Sharp-Shooters," *Republican*, August 17, 1864.
256. "Fatal Accident," *Republican*, August 24, 1864.
257. "Second U.S. Sharp Shooters," *Republican*, September 7, 1864.
258. "2nd U.S. Sharpshooters," *Republican*, December 21, 1864.
259. "2nd U.S. Sharpshooters," *Republican*, December 28, 1864.
260. "Our Boys Are Coming Home," *Republican*, July 12, 1865.

Chapter 8

261. "Elder's Zouaves," *Republican*, June 19, 1861.
262. General Assembly, *Official Roster*, 436.
263. Bryanton, *Ingham County Directory*, 16.
264. "Elder's Zouaves," *Republican*, August 7, 1861.
265. Wilcox, "Capt. Abraham Cottrell," 11.
266. *Men of Progress*, 267.
267. "Filled Up," *Republican*, September 4, 1861.
268. Michigan Adjutant-General's Department, *Record of Service*, vol. 8, 9.
269. United States Federal Census, 1860, Lansing.
270. Bagley Family Papers, letter to Bagley from Elder, August 20, 1861.
271. "Departure of Elder's Zouaves," *Republican*, August 28, 1861.
272. Ibid.
273. "Camp Anderson," *Republican*, September 15, 1861.
274. "From Elder's Zouaves," *Republican*, November 20, 1861.
275. Wilcox, "Capt. Abraham Cottrell," 11.
276. Bingham, *Michigan Biographies*, vol. 2, 274–75.
277. Bagley Family Papers, letter to Bagley from Tillinghast Brownell, January 31, 1864.
278. Baker, letter to Harvey Baker from Elder, March 15, 1862.
279. "Personal," *Republican*, April 30, 1862.
280. Wilcox, "Capt. Abraham Cottrell," 11.
281. "Michigan Eighth," *Republican*, July 2, 1862.
282. Michigan Adjutant-General's Department, *Record of Service*, vol. 8, 1.
283. "Eighth Regt. Mich Infantry, Vol's," *Republican*, December 10, 1862.
284. Michigan Adjutant-General's Department, *Record of Service*, vol. 8, 34.
285. "Resolution to Capt. Cottrell," *Republican*, April 8, 1863.
286. "From the Michigan 8th Regiment," *Republican*, June 3, 1863.

287. Heiser, "Sergeant George W.H. Stouch."
288. "Death of Lieut. M. Elder," *Republican*, July 29, 1863.
289. "Death of Sibley J. Ingersoll," *Republican*, November 11, 1863.
290. "From the Eighth Michigan Infantry," *Republican*, April 27, 1864.
291. "The Virginia Battle Field," *Republican*, May 25, 1864.
292. Ibid.
293. "Death of Rev. Edward Flower," *St. Joseph, Missouri Gazette*, September 5, 1911.
294. "Recruiting," *Republican*, August 10, 1864.
295. "Dear Friend Foster," *Republican*, December 7, 1864.
296. "Returned Co. 'E,'" *Republican*, August 23, 1865.

Chapter 9

297. Smith, *Michigan Pioneer Collections*, vol. 6, 286.
298. Ibid., 284.
299. "Michigan Female College," *Republican*, September 7, 1864.
300. Smith, *Michigan Pioneer Collections*, vol. 6, 286.
301. Ibid.
302. "The Female College-Report of the Conference Visitors," *Republican*, July 31, 1861.
303. Ibid.
304. Ibid.
305. "Commencement at Michigan Female College," *Republican*, July 9, 1862.
306. "Michigan Soldiers Relief Association," *Republican*, April 12, 1865.

Chapter 10

307. Ruff, *Michigan History Magazine*, vol. 27, 281.
308. "To Our Readers," *Republican*, October 23, 1861.
309. Ibid.
310. United States Federal Census, 1850, Washtenaw County and 1860, Lansing.
311. *Republican*, June 18, 1862.
312. United States Federal Census, 1860, Eaton County; Michigan Adjutant-General's Department, *Record of Service*, vol. 12, 88.

313. "Captain Cravath's Company," *Republican*, November 6, 1861.
314. "Sword Presentation," *Republican*, February 5, 1862.
315. "Twelfth Regiment," *Republican*, February 12, 1862.
316. Ruff, *Michigan History Magazine*, vol. 27, 282.
317. "From the Twelfth Michigan Regiment," *Republican*, April 16, 1862.
318. Chernow, *Grant*, 196.
319. Ibid.
320. Ruff, *Michigan History Magazine*, vol. 27, 289.
321. "From the 12th Michigan Regiment," *Republican*, October 8, 1862.
322. Chernow, *Grant*, 201.
323. "Captain Cravath," *Republican*, April 30, 1862.
324. Ibid.
325. "A Returned Prisoner," *Republican*, April 1, 1863.
326. "From the Twelfth Michigan Regiment," *Republican*, June 25, 1862.
327. "Captain Cravath," *Republican*, May 21, 1862.
328. "Capt. Cravath," *Republican*, June 4, 1862.
329. Circus fans of America, historical marker at Adado Park, Lansing, Michigan.
330. "The Lansing State Republican," *Republican*, May 30, 1866.
331. "Letter from Mr. Cravath," *Republican*, February 3, 1864.
332. Library of Michigan, Michigan Legislative Biography Database.
333. Reports of Committees, 48th Congress, 2nd Session.
334. "Corporal Strong at Home," *Republican*, April 30, 1862; "An Opportunity," May 21, 1862.
335. *Republican*, June 18, 1862.
336. "Died," *Republican*, October 1, 1862.
337. "Providential," *Republican*, October 8, 1862.
338. "Resigned," *Republican*, April 29, 1863.
339. United States Federal Census, 1910, Cook County, Illinois; Cook County, Illinois, Death Index, 1908–1988.
340. Robertson, *Michigan in the War*, 326.
341. Myers, "Twelfth Michigan Volunteer Infantry," 29–47.
342. Michigan Adjutant-General's Department, *Record of Service*, vol. 12, 165.
343. "Married," *Republican*, December 14, 1864.
344. Michigan Adjutant-General's Department, *Record of Service*, vol. 12, 165.
345. "Joseph C. Wardell," *Detroit Free Press*, March 18, 1931.
346. "The 12th Mich. Infantry," *Republican*, March 7, 1866.

Chapter 11

347. *Annual Report,* 5.
348. Ibid., 30.
349. "For the Reform School," *Republican,* August 30, 1859.
350. "Mich. State Reform School," *Republican,* January 7, 1863.
351. "State Reform School," *Republican,* January 8, 1862; January 22, 1862.
352. Foster, *Descendants of Theodore Foster,* 85.
353. Ibid., 86.
354. Thavenet, "Michigan Reform School," 21–46.
355. Ibid., 22–23.
356. McCormick, "From Inmates to Infantrymen,"1. [page numbers?].
357. Thavenet, "Michigan Reform School," 28.
358. "Thanksgiving at the Reform School," *Republican,* December 4, 1861.
359. McCormick, "From Inmates to Infantrymen," 1.
360. Thavenet, "From Inmates to Infantrymen," 32.
361. "Mich. State Reform School," *Republican,* January 7, 1863.
362. "Reform School Boys," *Republican,* August 23, 1865.

Chapter 12

363. Thavenet, "From Inmates to Infantrymen," table 2, 35.
364. Robertson, *Michigan in the War,* 491.
365. McCormick, "Reckoning," 19.

Chapter 13

366. "But Ten Veterans of The Lansing Rangers Present at Reunion," *Journal,* September 26, 1914.
367. "Lansing Rangers," *Republican,* February 5, 1862.
368. "Jeffrie's Rangers," *Republican,* January 8, 1862.
369. *Portrait and Biographical Album,* 403–4.
370. "Notes from Camp—No. 2," *Republican,* April 9, 1862.
371. "Uncle Dan Mevis, Pioneer and Scribe of Early Lansing, Dies," *Journal,* December 12, 1930.
372. "Notes from Camp—No. 1," *Journal,* March 19, 1862.
373. "Notes from Camp—No. 3," *Journal,* May 28, 1862.

374. "Death of Capt. Jas. J. Jeffres [*sic*], 14th Mich. Infantry.," *Journal*, August 3, 1864.

375. Michigan Adjutant-General's Department, *Record of Service*, vol. 14, 1–3.

376. *Portrait and Biographical Album*. 403–4.

Chapter 14

377. United States Federal Census, 1860, Lansing.

378. *Joint Documents*, 19, 23.

379. "Departure of Capt. Weber's Company," *Republican*, August 21, 1861.

380. United States Federal Census, 1860, Lansing.

381. "From Stockton's Regiment," *Republican*, February 12, 1862.

382. "From Stockton's Regiment," *Republican*, May 14, 1862.

383. "From Stockton's Regiment," *Republican*, July 23, 1862.

384. Ibid.

385. Ibid.

386. United States Federal Census, 1860, Lansing.

387. "Volunteer," *Republican*, December 17, 1862.

388. *Lansing State Republican*, July 2, 1879.

389. *Republican*, November 9, 1864.

Chapter 15

390. Cutcheon, *Twentieth Michigan Infantry*, 11.

391. United States Federal Census, 1860, Lansing.

392. "Major A.W. Williams," *Republican*, August 7, 1861.

393. Michigan Adjutant-General's Department, *Record of Service*, vol. 20, 183.

394. "Personal," *Republican*, July 9, 1862.

395. "Recruiting," *Republican*, August 6, 1862.

396. "The Ingham County Company," *Republican*, August 13, 1862.

397. *Republican*, August 20, 1862.

398. Ibid.

399. Ibid.

400. United States Federal Census, 1860, Lansing.

401. Ibid.

402. Mosher and Beane, "Beginning of Public Health," 16.

403. Ibid.

404. Weible, "Leoni Was Home."

405. "Dr. Orville P. Chubb."

406. "Dr. Chubb," *Republican*, June 29, 1864.

407. Michigan Adjutant-General's Department, *Record of Service*, vol. 20, 27.

408. "Dr. Orville P. Chubb."

409. *Republican*, August 27, 1862.

410. United States Federal Census, 1860, Lansing.

411. "Presentation to Capt. Smith," *Republican*, September 3, 1862.

412. Ibid.

413. "Camp Items," *Republican*, September 17, 1862.

414. Ibid.

415. Ibid.

416. "Washington Correspondence," *Republican*, September 17, 1862.

417. Ibid.

418. "Camp Items," *Republican*, October 1, 1862.

419. Ibid.

420. "Camp Items," *Republican*, October 15, 1862.

421. Ibid.

422. "Camp Items," *Republican*, November 26, 1862.

423. Ibid.

424. Ibid.

425. Michigan Adjutant-General's Department, *Record of Service*, vol. 20, 36.

426. "From the Michigan 20th Regt.," *Republican*, December 3, 1862.

427. "Resolutions of Torrent Engine Co. No. 1 on the death of Harmon W. Paddleford," *Republican*, January 3, 1863.

428. "Died," *Republican*, December 10, 1862.

429. "The Soldiers' Funerals," *Republican*, December 31, 1862.

430. Ibid.

431. Roach, *Stiff*, 79–80.

432. "Embalming the Dead," *Republican*, October 8, 1862.

433. Cutcheon, *Twentieth Michigan Infantry*, 44.

434. "Letter From Col A.W. Williams.," *Republican*, February 4, 1863.

435. "Died," *Republican*, April 1, 1863.

436. Michigan Adjutant-General's Department, *Record of Service*, vol. 20, 52.

437. "A Week of Accidents," *Republican*, October 14, 1863.
438. Michigan Adjutant-General's Department, *Record of Service*, vol. 20, 102.
439. Farnsworth, *Southern California Paradise*, 59.
440. Sadler, *Frontier Days in Crescenta Valley*, 59.
441. "Adolphus Wesley Williams," Find a Grave.
442. Cutcheon, *Twentieth Michigan Infantry*, 61.
443. Ibid., 54.
444. "A Sad Announcement," *Republican*, May 13, 1863.
445. Foster, *Descendants of Theodore Foster*, 91.
446. Michigan Pioneer and Historical Society, *Historical Collections*, vol. 36, 655.
447. "Judge Albert E. Cowles," *Ingham County Democrat*, November 28, 1906.
448. Cutcheon, *Twentieth Michigan Infantry*, 75.
449. "Presentation to Capt. Smith," *Republican*, September 3, 1862.
450. "Dr. Chubb," *Republican*, June 29, 1864.
451. "Letter from Capt. Dewey," *Republican*, June 29, 1864.
452. Ibid.
453. "Before Petersburg," *Republican*, August 3, 1864.
454. "Col. Cutcheon," *Republican*, August 24, 1864.
455. Ibid.
456. Michigan Adjutant-General's Department, *Record of Service*, vol. 20, 57, 45.
457. "Furloughed," *Republican*, February 22, 1865.
458. United States Federal Census, 1850, Lincoln Township, Ohio.
459. Cutcheon, *Twentieth Michigan Infantry*, 271.

Chapter 16

460. United States Federal Census, 1860, Lansing.
461. "Married," *Republican*, December 12, 1860.
462. "Annual Election of Hook and Ladder Co. No. 1.," *Republican*, October 16, 1861; "Masonic Election," *Republican*, December 18, 1861; "Lincoln Wide-Awake Club," *Republican*, June 13, 1860.
463. Herek, *These Men Have Seen*, 11.
464. Michigan Adjutant-General's Department, *Record of Service*, vol. 44, 45.
465. "Pure Patriotism," *Republican*, October 21, 1863.

466. Michigan Adjutant-General's Department, *Record of Service*, vol. 44, 2.

467. "In Town," *Republican*, November 18, 1863.

468. "Letter from Mr. Cravath," *Republican*, February 3, 1864.

469. "First Michigan Sharp-Shooters," *Republican*, July 6, 1864.

470. Herek, *These Men Have Seen*, 279.

471. "The Army of the Potomac," *Republican*, February 15, 1865.

472. Herek, *These Men Have Seen*, 317.

473. "Suicide of Col. A.W. Nichols," *Republican*, January 24, 1866.

474. Herek, *These Men Have Seen*, 367.

Chapter 17

475. "Proceedings in the City," *Republican*, April 19, 1865.

476. "Funeral Exercises," *Republican*, April 26, 1865.

477. "Our Boys Are Coming Home," *Republican*, June 7, 1865.

478. "My Boys Not Coming Home," *Republican*, June 21, 1865.

479. Foster, *Descendants of Theodore Foster*, 92.

480. "The New Pension Law," *Republican*, June 27, 1866.

Bibliography

Acts of the Legislature of the State of Michigan, Passed at the Regular Session of 1855 […]. Lansing, MI: Geo. W. Peck, 1855. https://www.google.com/books/edition/Public_and_Local_Acts_of_the_Legislature/bmCqjTw6D0IC.

Adam, Mrs. Franc L. *The Pioneer History of Ingham County*. Vol. 1. Lansing, MI: Wynkoop, Hallenbeck, Crawford, 1923.

"Adolphus Wesley Williams." Find a Grave. https://www.findagrave.com/memorial/7920809/adolphus-wesley-williams.

Army, Thomas F. Jr., *Engineering Victory: How Technology Won the Civil War*. Baltimore, MD: Johns Hopkins University Press, 2016, 86. www.google.com/books/edition/Engineering_Victory/.

Bagley Family Papers. Collection Identifier 00018, Michigan State University Archives and Historical Collections, East Lansing, Michigan.

Bak, Richard. *A Distant Thunder: Michigan in the Civil War*. Ann Arbor, MI: Huron River Press, 2004.

Baker, James H. The Baker Collection. Clements Library, University of Michigan.

Ballard, D. La Pierre. "The Appleton Ballard Family of Lansing, Michigan." January 30, 2016. http://www.balcro.com/ballard.html.

Barnett, Le Roy G. "The History of a Sample Michigan Land Grant, 1873–1920." *Michigan Historical Review* 47, no. 1 (2001): 1–28. https://doi.org/10.1353/mhr.2021.0001.

Bingham, Stephen D. *Michigan Biographies*. Vol. 2. Lansing: Michigan Historical Commission, 1924.

Blackburn, George, ed. *With the Wandering Regiment: The Diary of Captain Ralph Ely of the Eighth Michigan Infantry.* Mount Pleasant: Central Michigan University Press, 1965.

Bryanton, Mike. *2011–2012 Ingham County Directory.* Mason, MI: Ingham County Clerk.

Castro, Manuel. "The Man Who Died Twice." *Metropolitan Quarterly,* October 1990.

Chernow, Ron. *Grant.* New York: Penguin Press, 2017.

Christen, William. *Stonewall Regiment: A History of the 17th Michigan Volunteer Infantry Regiment.* Detroit: 17th Michigan Volunteer Infantry Regiment, 1986.

Clark, Charles F. *Michigan State Gazetteer and Business Directory for Michigan,* Charles F. Clark, 1863.

Committee on the Impact of the Civil War upon the Lives of Women in Michigan. *Michigan Women in the Civil War.* Lansing: Michigan Civil War Centennial Observance Commission, 1963.

Cook County, Illinois, Death Index, 1908–1988.

Cowles, Albert E. *Past and Present of the City of Lansing and Ingham County, Michigan.* Lansing: Michigan Historical Publishing Association, 1905.

Crawford, Kim. *The 16th Michigan Infantry.* Dayton, OH: Morningside, 2002.

Cutcheon, Byron M. *The Story of the Twentieth Michigan Infantry.* Lansing, MI: Robert Smith Printing, 1904.

Daboll, Sherman B., and Kelley, Dean W. *Past and Present of Clinton County, Michigan.* Chicago: S.J. Clarke, 1906.

Demographia. "US Population History from 1850: 50 Largest Cities." http://www.demographia.com/db-uscity1850.htm.

Dempsey, Jack, and Egen, Brian J. *Michigan at Antietam.* Charleston, SC: The History Press, 2015.

Edmonds, J.P. *Early Lansing History.* Lansing: F. Dekleine, 1944.

Elliott, Frank N. "Transportation in Lansing." Paper presented before the Lansing Historical Society, April 2, 1959.

Ellison, Garret. "Remembering the 1,040-Man West Michigan Regiment Who Fought in the Civil War 150 Years Ago." MLive, April 3, 2019. https://www.mlive.com/news/grand-rapids/2011/06/remembering_the_1040-man_west.html.

Farnsworth, R.W.C. *A Southern California Paradise (In the Suburbs of Los Angeles): Being a Historic and Descriptive Account of Pasadena, San Gabriel, Sierra Madre, and La Cañada; With Important Reference to Los Angeles and All Southern California.* Pasadena, CA: R.W.C. Farnsworth, 1883.

First Annual Report of the Board of Control of the House of Correction for Juvenile Offenders of the State of Michigan. Lansing, MI: Hosmer and Kerr, 1858.

Foster, Lille. *Some Michigan Descendants of Theodore Foster.* A Family Tree Maker Smart Story: 2019.

The General Assembly, *Official Roster of the Soldiers of the State of Ohio in War of the Rebellion and in the War with Mexico,* vol. 12, Norwalk, Ohio: The Laning Company, 1895.

Heiser, John. "Sergeant George W.H. Stouch Returns to Gettysburg." *From the Fields of Gettysburg: The Blog of Gettysburg National Military Park,* June 19, 2015, https://npsgnmp.wordpress.com/2015/06/19/sergeant-stouch-returns-to-gettysburg/.

Herek, Raymond J. *These Men Have Seen Hard Service: The First Michigan Sharpshooters in the Civil War.* Detroit, MI: Wayne State University Press, 1998.

Hoffman, Mark. *"My Brave Mechanics": The First Michigan Engineers and Their Civil War.* Detroit, MI: Wayne State University Press, 2007.

Joint Documents of the State of Michigan for the Year 1860. Lansing, MI: Hosmer and Kerr, 1861.

Lawler, Jerry. "Origin of the City of Lansing." Unpublished manuscript from the Capitol Chronology series, 2005.

Library of Michigan. Michigan Legislative Biography Database. https://mdoe.state.mi.us/legislators.

Martin County Minnesota Historical Society. "Dr. Orville P. Chubb—Pioneer Physician of Martin County." Accessed October 21, 2021. http://www.fairmont.org/mchs/Dr.%20Orville%20P.%20Chubb.pdf.

McCormick, David. "From Inmates to Infantrymen: The Michigan Boys' Reform School and the American Civil War." Retrieved September 29, 2022. https://www.thefreelibrary.com/FROM+IN MATES+TO+INFANTRYMEN%3A+The+Michigan+Boys%27+Reform+School+and+the...-a0521291017.

McCormick, Jacob. "Reckoning with a Troubled Past: The John Taylor Lynching." *Chronicle, Historical Society of Michigan* 44, no. 1 (Spring 2021).

McRae, Norman. *Negroes in Michigan during the Civil War.* Lansing: Michigan Civil War Centennial Observance Commission, 1966.

Men of Progress Embracing Biographical Sketches of Representative Michigan. Detroit, MI: Evening News Association, 1900.

Michigan Adjutant-General's Department. *Record of Service of Michigan Volunteers in the Civil War, 1861–1865.* 46 vols. Kalamazoo, MI: Ihling Brothers & Everard, 1905.

Michigan Department of Transportation. *Michigan's Railroad History 1825–2014*. Michigan Department of Transportation: October 2014. https://www.michigan.gov/-/media/Project/Websites/MDOT/Travel/Mobility/Rail/Michigan-Railroad-History.pdf.

Michigan History Magazine. Michigan Historical Commission. Lansing, Michigan: Vol. 9, 1925.

Michigan Pioneer and Historical Society. *Historical Collections*. 40 vols. Lansing, MI: Wynkoop, Hallenbeck, Crawford, 1912.

Michigan Soldiers and Sailors Alphabetical Index. Lansing, MI: Wynkoop, Hallenbeck, Crawford, 1915.

Michigan, U.S., County Marriage Records, 1822–1940, Ancestry.com.

Michigan, U.S., Death Records, 1867–1952, Ancestry.com. [database on-line]. Provo, UT, USA: Ancestry.com Operations, Inc., 2015.

Millbrook, Minnie. *A Study in Valor; Michigan Medal of Honor Winners in the Civil War*. Lansing: Michigan Civil War Centennial Observance Commission, 1966.

Mosher, Robert E., and G.E. Beane. "The Beginning of Public Health in Michigan." *Michigan Journal of Public Health* 2, no. 1 (2008): 12.

Myers, Robert C. "Mortality in the Twelfth Michigan Volunteer Infantry, 1861–1866." *Michigan Historical Review* 20, no. 1 (Spring 1994), 29–47. https://doi.org/10.2307/20173432.

Official Roster of the Soldiers of the State of Ohio in War of the Rebellion and in the War with Mexico. Vol. 12. Norwalk, OH: Laning Company, 1895.

Portrait and Biographical Album of Ingham and Livingston Counties, Michigan Containing Biographical Sketches of Prominent and Representative Citizens of the Counties, Together with Biographies of All the Governors of the State, and of the Presidents of the United States. Chicago: Chapman Brothers, 1891.

Records of Internment in the Seven Pines National Cemetery. Section A, U.S. Department of Veterans Affairs, https://gravelocator.cem.va.gov/.

Report of Committees of the Senate of the United States for the First Session of the Forty-Fourth Congress, 1875–'76. 3 vols. Washington, D.C.: Government Printing Office, 1876. https://www.google.com/books/edition/Reports_of_Committees/ArQFAAAAQAAJ.

Roach, Mary. *Stiff: The Curious Lives of Human Cadavers*. New York: W.W. Norton, 2003.

Robertson, John. *Michigan in the War*. Lansing: W.S. George, 1882.

Roosevelt. Theodore. "A Very Sad Thing," Theodore Roosevelt: Letters and Speeches, Library of America, https://storyoftheweek.loa.org/2019/02/a-very-sad-thing.html

Ruff, Joseph. *Michigan History Magazine*. Vol. 27, Lansing, Michigan Historical Commission, 1943.

Sadler, Jo Anne. *Frontier Days in Crescenta Valley: Portraits of Life in the Foothills*. Charleston, SC: The History Press, 2014.

Seidman, Rachel Filene. "'We Were Enlisted for the War': Ladies' Aid Societies and the Politics of Women's Work During the Civil War," in *Making and Remaking Pennsylvania's Civil War*, edited by William Blair and William Pencak. University Park: Pennsylvania State University Press, 2001.

Smith, Eliza C. *Michigan Pioneer Collections*. Vol. 6. Lansing, MI, Wynkoop, Hallenbeck, Crawford, 1907.

Soper, Steve. *The "Glorious Old Third": A History of the Third Michigan Infantry 1855 to 1927*. Self-published, Third Michigan Publications, 2011.

Stevens, C.A. [Charles Augustus]. *Berdan's United States Sharpshooters in the Army of the Potomac, 1861–1865*. St. Paul, MN: Price-McGill, 1892.

Stille, Charles J. *History of the United States Sanitary Commission: Being the General Report of Its Work During the War of the Rebellion*. Philadelphia: J.B. Lippincott & Co., 1866. p. 63.

Thavenet, Dennis. "The Michigan Reform School and the Civil War: Officers and Inmates Mobilized for the Union Cause," *Michigan Historical Review* no 1 (Spring 1987): 21–46.

Tinder, David V. *Directory of Early Photographers*. William L. Clements Library, University of Michigan, online edition. https://clements.umich.edu/files/tinder_directory.pdf.

Tomek, Beverly C. "Women and Soldiers' Aid Societies." *Essential Civil War Curriculum*, June 2019. https://www.essentialcivilwarcurriculum.com/women-and-soldiers-aid-societies.html.

United States Federal Census. 1860, Eaton County, Michigan.

———. 1850, Lincoln Township, Ohio.

———. 1850, Madison Township, Richland County, Ohio.

———. 1850, Washtenaw County, Michigan.

———. 1860, Lansing, Ingham, Michigan. Roll M653_545.

———. 1910, Cook County, Illinois.

United States War Department et al. *The War of the Rebellion: A Compilation of the Official Records of the Union and Confederate Armies*. 1880 Official Report no. 28; series 1, volume 2 (serial no. 2). Washington, D.C.: Government Printing Office, 1880–1901. https://www.loc.gov/item/03003452/.

Veteran. Save the Flags Records, Third Michigan Binder, 1884.

"Weapons of the Civil War." *Life Explores: History of the Rifle: The Weapon That Changed the World* (2021).

Weible, Susanne. "Leoni Was Home to Bustling College." *Jackson Citizen Patriot*, September 10, 2007.

Whitman, John J. "Last Will and Testament of John J. Whitman," September 28, 1861, Michigan Wills and Probate Records 1784–1980, via Ancestry.com. https://www.ancestry.com/search/collections/8793/.

Wilbur, C.K. *Civil War Medicine*. Guilford, CT: Globe Pequot Press, 1998.

Wilcox, Kean. "Capt. Abraham Cottrell: The Life of a Soldier-Photographer." *Military Images* 7, no. 5 (March 1986): 11.

Newspapers

Detroit Advertiser and Tribune
Detroit Free Press
Grand Rapids Enquirer
Lansing State Republican
State Journal
St. Joseph, Missouri Gazette

About the Author

Born and raised in Lansing, Matthew J. VanAcker is the director and curator of Save the Flags, a project to research, display and conserve 240 battle flags carried by Michigan soldiers in the Civil War, the Spanish-American War and World War I. He also serves as the director of the Michigan State Capitol Tour and Education Service and as vice president of the Michigan Civil War Association. He has spoken and written extensively about the Michigan state capitol and the Capitol Battle Flag Collection. He resides in West Lansing with his wife, Mary Kathleen, in an 1885 farmhouse where they raised their four children.